B4B

How Technology and Big Data Are Reinventing the Customer-Supplier Relationship

J.B. Wood
Todd Hewlin
Thomas Lah

Contents

Introduction (Important!)

So how do you get 300 global technology suppliers to work together on a single challenge—in this case, the challenge being business model transformation? It's not that high-tech and near-tech industries are replacing the traditional product business model we are all used to; they are just struggling to add a profitable "as-a-service" business model to it.

This book presents a narrative more than a theory. It chronicles the industry shifts and discusses how they are leading, at least in our view, to a logical conclusion. That conclusion is simple, yet fundamental: The product B2B model was designed to sell things *to* customers, whereas the new B4B model will be about delivering outcomes *for* customers. This one simple statement will lead to a fundamental change in the thinking of both suppliers and their customers. Change isn't always easy for executives. Sometimes you have to believe that people, organizations, and companies can play roles you never thought they could play. Sometimes you have to take a deep breath when you realize that your company may be completely missing critical capabilities, or that entire organizations must be redirected or resized. If you are a tech supplier, at some point you have to consider whether adding feature number

1,723 and sales rep number 1,634 are still the best investments. This change will require you to consider all of the above.

It is important to note that this book was not just written by the authors or by a single supplier that had a vested interest in the message. Instead, we wrote this book from the thousands of dialogues we have had with those 300 suppliers, complemented by conversations with hundreds of business customers.

Change is coming. Of that there is no doubt. For suppliers, optimizing their product-attached services business probably represents the short-term solution to the growth problems that will confront them this year and next. In the longer term, we hope the direction proposed in this book provides the strategic answers that the industry seems to be struggling to clarify. We are the Technology Services Industry Association, and we think it is our job to leverage our unique platform that connects leading suppliers with our world-class research experts to lead the debate about service business models. Tech suppliers can choose to figure things out for themselves, of course. But most suppliers we know are so busy peddling harder, trying to keep the old business model growing, that they don't have much time to think about the new one. Instead, they should join the industrywide discussion. That is exactly how 300 global companies are going to accelerate their transformation: by coming together to work on a single challenge—one that may likely determine their future.

—*JW, TH, TL*

1 | The Origins of B2B

THE OPERATING MODEL THAT SITS BETWEEN THE COMPANIES WHO supply business technology and the customers who buy it is about to be revolutionized. The proof of this premise is already presenting itself in the financial statements of suppliers from Amazon to Xerox. When the dust settles, neither party in the technology market equation will be untouched—and these days, what part of business isn't about technology?

The Pesky Disruptor

On August 20, 2011, an editorial appeared in the *Wall Street Journal*. The headline read "Why Software Is Eating the World," and it was written by Silicon Valley legend Marc Andreessen. What Mr. Andreessen had to say was something simple, yet profound: It seemed to him that software, and specifically software run over the Internet, was finally achieving its potential.

As he saw it, this meant that software was playing not only its traditional role of improving the productivity of companies. It was also disrupting and dislocating some of them. It was not stopping there, however. It was now doing unthinkable things such as figuring out how to eat products that used to be physical products. And perhaps most provocative was that this brash and irreverent technology was rapidly jumping its traditional fences. It wasn't just eating the tech industry; it was eating *many* industries.

It's hard to argue with Andreessen's logic. Just look around the world of business today. It's hard to find an industry that is immune to this pesky disruptor. Not too long ago, physical products that were physically distributed dominated the world of business (see Figures 1.1 and 1.2).

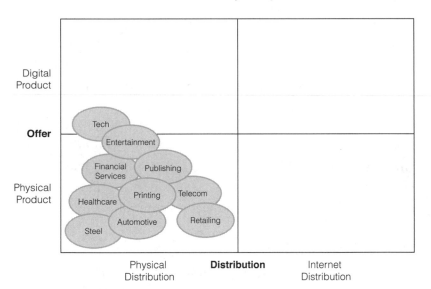

Before the Pesky Disruptor

FIGURE 1.1 Before the Pesky Disruptor

By this definition of physicality, even the high-tech industry was not truly digital until the last decade. More than half the industry's revenue came from hardware—a physical product that was physically distributed to customers. And although the software that ran on it was truly digital, it was demonstrated on-site by a salesperson and then physically shipped on CDs or sold to consumers in shrink-wrapped boxes at local stores. Everything was that way. You went to a video store to rent movies on CDs. You went into the bank to transfer money. If you wanted your medical records, you went to your doctor's office to pick up your files. And then,

How "Software Is Eating the World"

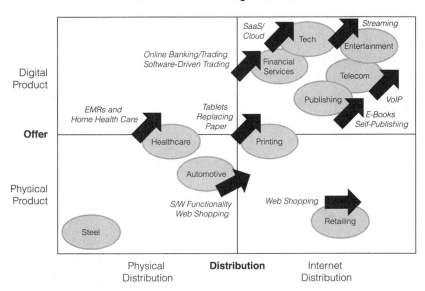

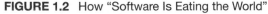

FIGURE 1.2 How "Software Is Eating the World"

to *really* summarize Andreessen's point, the "software big bang" happened.

Dozens of industries have already felt the epic force of the software big bang. Andreessen argues that this is because, for the first time in history, the global economy is becoming truly digitally connected. This includes not only people with devices and companies with computers, but also industrial equipment and machines that talk to one another. This is enabling software and the Internet to play disruptive roles not just in the lives of consumers, but in almost every vertical and horizontal business-to-business (B2B) industry as well.

It is the rise of "near-tech." Medical device and telecommunication product providers crossed over years ago from offering mechanical and analog solutions to their business customers. Now, embedded hardware, software, and sensor networks are revolutionizing test and measurement products, ground transportation systems, aerospace, energy, and security systems. Software, robotics, and three-dimensional (3-D) printing have revolutionized manufacturing. Cars are now shipping with sensors and software that not only will automatically bring the cars to a complete stop from cruising speed but will also help the driver keep the car in the center of its lane. Nanotechnology is revolutionizing materials development, and genetic analysis is making the prescribing of individually tailored drugs possible. It is almost harder to point at a segment of B2B that's *not* becoming near-tech. Even steel is being sold in digital, online marketplaces.

The Consequences of Becoming a Software-Driven Industry

Software allows a supplier to envision and construct new capabilities rapidly and almost limitlessly. But these new capabilities have to be built, tested, implemented, trained, managed, and maintained. The underlying information technology (IT) or manufacturing systems that host and deliver these new capabilities must work together as an intricate, global web of devices and services. The employees who use them must change their skills and their business processes. As the new capabilities are rolled out, who does what, when, and why within a company's ecosystem often gets scrambled and reassembled. Change and complexity become a way of life.

As software begins to eat away at an industry sector, it brings with it many other forces. It is safe to say that these forces, like software itself, will not stay inside the fences of the traditional high-tech industry. They are playing out in near-tech too. In each case, it tends to upset the old balance of power. Manufacturers are sometimes slow to accept how much or how quickly software could erode their revenue model or could shift the value away from the physical device they make. That makes room for smaller but more innovative companies to take a share. Resellers are often slow to adapt to the impending changes in the value chain as more original equipment manufacturers (OEMs) offer web-based, direct-to-end-customer offers that threaten to disintermediate them. Product architectures and pricing models begin changing at uncomfortable rates. Industry sectors that have had stable, predictable market conditions for years can quickly be staring into an unfamiliar future—often benefiting new entrants with new approaches. It is not just a high-tech phenomenon anymore; the number of near-tech industries is exploding, and in each one, change is accelerating.

But there may be another force of change, one that has not yet been put into a useful context. As with many others, it will be prone to jumping industry fences.

In 2011, we published a book called *Consumption Economics*.[1] That book framed some important shifts at a time when trends were less certain than they are today. We picked seven dynamics, shown in Figure 1.3, that were emerging at different rates of speed in the tech industry but were evident enough at the time that we were confident in calling them out as "here to stay" forces.

The New Rules of Tech

1 Risk Shifts to the Vendor

2 Simplicity Will Be King

3 Users Drive Tech Decisions

4 Customer Aggregators Shrink Direct Market

5 Channel Value Reset

6 Tech Pricing Under Pressure

7 Behavioral Data Leverage

Source: *Consumption Economics*, 2011.

FIGURE 1.3 The New Rules of Tech

There is not much we would change today about these assertions. In fact, most of them are assertions no longer. There are plenty of proof points. We could call the trends early because we work with 300 global tech companies every day, and we get to hear what keeps them up every night. What is interesting is that these trends are having impacts on both sides of the commercial fence. By this we mean that they are changing the operating models of both business suppliers and their customers. Just pick an industry and look at how business within that industry is conducted today. Then think about how software, sensor networks, and big data analytics are beginning to change the way both parties in the commercial transaction are operating—who does what, how they interact, how they share risk and reward. We think we are approaching a point of fundamental change in how business customers partner with their suppliers—in effect, how B2B works.

The Current B2B Model

Before we can think forward, we need to chart the basic structure of today's B2B operating model. We need to model a "before" picture so we can contrast it to the "after" model. That made us begin to wonder: Just how did the current B2B operating model develop?

That question led us to a pretty surprising answer. We think that the basic B2B operating model—the one that is in place today between thousands of product suppliers and millions of business customers—can be largely traced to the thoughts and actions of a single individual. At least as surprising is that it was designed not 40 years ago or even 60 years ago. The B2B operating model most often practiced today was actually designed in the 1880s, more than 125 years ago.

But first we need to set some context. Let's start with something that one might readily agree is an obvious, immutable fact: There has always been a natural divide between the fundamental self-interest of a supplier and the fundamental self-interest of any of its potential customers, as shown in Figure 1.4.

FIGURE 1.4 The B2B Divide

Let's start with the customer. On any given day, a company who is a potential B2B customer wants to figure out how to make more money. It seeks to build a better product, improve the skills of its workforce, design a more efficient business process, and/or outperform a competitor. It is a never-ending process for a well-run company. It constantly and vigilantly scans for opportunities to improve its operating and financial outcomes. In addition to its own internal improvements, a company knows that a world of suppliers exists that may have product or service offerings that could help the company reach its goals better, faster, or cheaper than it could do alone. Thus, companies regularly partner with suppliers and pay them in order to achieve an improved outcome.

Suppliers, on the other hand, wake up each day with a slightly different motivation. They have made an investment. It could be in factories, it could be in material, it could be in people, or it could be in all of them. They have invested in manufacturing an inventory of product assets that they need to move off their balance sheet at a profit. They need to find potential customers who may be interested in procuring those assets at the targeted selling price. In short, when suppliers wake up in the morning, they are thinking about a supply of product assets that needs to be pushed into the market. That is what they focus on.

The dance between these two parties goes on every day in the business world: suppliers wanting to push their products or services into the market and potential customers wanting to improve their outcomes. The trick has always been how to most efficiently bridge the divide in a way that is successful for both parties. For the customer, the objective is to isolate and partner with the *right* supplier, one that really improves their outcomes. For the supplier, the objective is to sell the most products. This dance is hardly new. No doubt it has been going on as far back as civilization began trading.

It was certainly the case in the booming United States of America in the 1880s. With the US Civil War finally settled, the South being rebuilt, westward expansion flourishing, and the Second Industrial Revolution generating breakthroughs in transportation and factory output, the US economy was in its "Gilded Age." It was the greatest period of economic growth in US history. This was the age of the tycoon, a period during which capital investment was increasing at a tremendous rate. And none of it escaped the watchful, wishful eye of Mr. John H. Patterson.

In 1884 at the age of 40, John Patterson bought controlling interest in a 13-employee maker of cash registers called the National Manufacturing Company of Dayton, Ohio, for $6,500.[2] At that time, it is believed that there were fewer than 400 cash registers in use in the United States.[3] Patterson had become one of those early owners after becoming suspicious that a clerk in his coal business was taking cash from him. He bought a cash register to provide him an accurate accounting of each day's receipts.[4]

After what is believed to be a brief period of buyer's remorse (he is thought to have asked for his $6,500 back), he set about taking control of the company. He changed the name to the National Cash Register Company (NCR) and began to focus on its numerous challenges, including limited capacity, manufacturing quality problems, and weak sales. It was his focus on that last category that would make him one of the most important business figures in the post-industrial age—a man whom some would later call the "father of professional selling."[5]

From the beginning, Patterson was passionate about the potential for his new technology category. He turned out to be right. "In the late nineteenth century and early twentieth, the invention of the typewriter, cash register, and adding machine changed the daily routine of the secretary, shop clerk, accountant, and bank teller. With their speed and accuracy, these and other small business machines were the computers of their day. More than mere appliances, they came to symbolize the essence of modern business practice."[6] Although broadly embraced as an essential business technology tool in fewer than 25 years (NCR sold more than 80,000 cash registers in 1910), the early days of NCR required Patterson to be bold and innovative to sell something that few customers believed they needed.

You see, in the 1880s, selling in the B2B world was largely the domain of independent representatives who carried many goods from many companies. The Industrial Revolution had spawned a new breed of manufacturer that could produce more products than could be sold and consumed in markets that were local to its factories. Hence, a model for broader geographic distribution was needed, and independent reps sprang up to fill that void. Often these independent reps carried multiple, directly competitive products at once in order to improve their chances of making sales. They relied on catalogs and order forms as the tools of their trade. Despite being poorly trained and often less than scrupulous, these reps offered affordable geographic sales coverage to product companies. This was the standard distribution model of its day, and John H. Patterson knew very early on that it would *not* work for NCR.

Patterson appeared to base this decision on two fundamental challenges, both of which had to do with complexity. First was the complexity of the product itself. The cash register was a modern marvel of its time. An effective salesperson would need to be able to explain its many features and even to operate the device in order to show off its capability. The second complexity lay in the nature of the selling. Shopkeepers, saloons, inns, and stores had been keeping their daily cash receipts in a drawer and recording sales on a ledger for hundreds of years. Most owners thought that process worked adequately. If NCR was to be successful, Patterson needed salespeople who could skillfully frame the business problem (in this case, theft, mistakes, and slow customer service) for a prospective buyer before they could present the NCR product. Making this all the more challenging—and thus making the need for impeccable sales execution all the more critical—was the high price of NCR's machines. These considerations led Patterson to conclude that the sales process for his new company was not going to be one that he could entrust to those he could not control and who would not or could not be trained. He needed a new, more modern operating model—one that could handle the complexity of his technology company's exciting new offer.

Over the next 20 years, John H. Patterson would not only build one of the most successful international companies of its day; he would also define how many manufacturing companies would sell and deliver for the next 125 years. In his need to overcome the challenges of a complex sale, he found a new way to bridge the divide between the product assets that his plant was manufacturing and the customers who wanted to improve their business outcomes. NCR began to build the first large-scale, international, direct sales force (see Figure 1.5).

In 1884, NCR Built a New Kind of Bridge

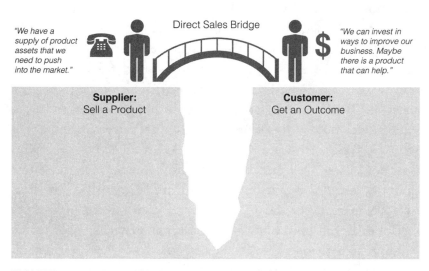

FIGURE 1.5 In 1884, NCR Built a New Kind of Bridge

Shortly after taking control, Patterson began to design and build his force of directly employed, full-time sales agents— trained, managed, and dedicated to sell NCR's products. Some were reps for manufacturers who already carried NCR as one of their products and whom he felt were up to the challenge of his new model. Others were from outside but were recruited to take on the job in areas not staffed. This was a real innovation in its day. But Patterson turned out not to be the type to congratulate himself on a big idea and leave the details up to someone else. He was a man who was compulsive, relentless, and controlling. He was not only going to be the new model's pioneer; he also was determined to perfect it. He innovated, refined, and progressed the sales operating model between a complex business product manufacturer and its customers.

The direct sales bridge between NCR and its customers was thoughtfully designed and managed. The two tower structures that (metaphorically) "held up" the NCR direct sales bridge were commissions and quotas. Commissions were already a well-known tactic for providing incentives to salespeople. In fact, most independent manufacturer reps of the day were 100% commission-based. What was relatively new was the addition and integration of defined, guaranteed territories with quotas. At first, quotas were set by the population in the territory, but they were eventually set by the territory's historical sales production.[7] By combining commissions and quotas into his direct sales model, he could not only provide incentive to salespeople who did well (commissions); he could also objectively tell who was not doing well and by how much (performance against quota). From this simple but elegant foundation, NCR went on to develop many of today's commonly used sales management tactics. It began publishing stack rankings of sales performance versus quota to motivate its agents, for example. It pioneered the use of sales contests and a "club" for top performers. It also developed elaborate, motivational sales conferences that closely resemble the "sales kickoff meetings" in place at most B2B companies today.

Patterson developed a science for not only motivating and managing his sales organization, but also professionalizing them. As we mentioned, he knew that the effectiveness of each sales call—the process, the proper framing of the prospect's business need, the product demo, and the closing tactics—was both delicate and critical. To control these variables, NCR salespeople were given scripts to memorize. The scripts were based on a four-part selling process. These became known collectively as the NCR Primer. As the product line grew more complex and the number of market segments increased, the number of scripts grew. This expanding body of codified sales practices led to yet more innovations. NCR is believed to have developed the first sales training school.[8] It was also among the first to test salespeople for their mastery of the NCR Primer.

NCR also revolutionized the B2B world through innovative marketing techniques. It was among the first, and certainly among the most sophisticated, in using B2B direct mail. The invention of customer testimonials is attributed to Patterson: "These testimonials proved among the strongest cases ever devised to sway prospects. They were 'living' arguments to buy."[9] NCR was an aggressive advertiser and developed a radically new, much simpler approach to business advertising that stressed visual simplicity and singularity of message over the busy, artsy standard of the day. NCR was even credited as being the first company to ever issue industrial press releases.

We were hardly the first to realize that Patterson was the designer of today's professional selling model. During Patterson's lifetime, scholars, authors, and motivators began writing about his achievements and have continued to do so. But after working with hundreds of global technology product companies, we do not think his impact stopped there. As NCR moved along its process of discovery around direct sales, Patterson also had to figure out how many other parts of the modern direct-to-business-customer model would work. We wish to assert that his design for the operations of NCR actually determined how B2B suppliers *think* today— determining how they operate far beyond just marketing and sales.

Let's take the lasting impact of a simple decision NCR made by assigning the job of collections to the salespeople. First, by requiring them to collect the money after the product had been delivered, he placed a kind of quality check on the deal. If what the customer received was not what the customer thought he or she had purchased, it was up to the salesperson to make that right. This encouraged salespeople to get the order right the first time. In a complex sale such as NCR's—especially as its line of models and options grew—Patterson likely knew that was a risk to be managed. But more important, by assigning salespeople *both* collections responsibility and a demanding quota, Patterson sent a second, more profound, message to his salespeople. He was telling them to get the sale, to get the order right, to get the money, and to *get out*. "On to the next deal!" he seemed to be telling them.

Today's modern B2B companies have evolved their deal quality controls. They install sophisticated "deal desks" inside their sales organizations or have expensive solution architects specifying the components that sales must include in the contract. These are the modern-day gates to mitigate the even greater risk of today's complex business solutions. The part of NCR's operating model that has not changed is the clear message most suppliers give to their salespeople about moving quickly from the last deal to the next one.

Because NCR didn't want its salespeople to stick around after the money was collected, it had to figure out who would. Most assuredly with a great deal of purpose, Patterson helped fuel another lasting B2B dynamic when he had a simple sign erected in the head office of the NCR service department: "We Cannot Afford to Have a Single Dissatisfied Customer."[10] As far as we can tell, there was no similar sign erected in the head office of the NCR sales department. It seems that Patterson had decided that sales would own the customer's revenue and service would own their satisfaction. This bifurcated approach to how most B2B suppliers think about their customer management activities remains alive and well in nearly every company we see. How cognizant NCR was of the distinction at the time or whether it was the first to draw it is immaterial. NCR added it to its operating model, and as we will soon learn, that operating model later proved to be really, really sticky.

Beyond sales and service, NCR also wrote the modern book on how to be a fierce competitor in the world of technology products. It refined the art not only of fiercely defending its patents, but also of tying up competition in costly patent infringement litigation. Patterson ordered that new models from competing companies be purchased indirectly and brought to Dayton to be torn apart. This not only gave him his legal targets, but it also allowed him to search out any true competitive innovations so that his engineers could begin to copy or improve them. He had squads of specially trained and skilled salespeople called "knockers" who were put into any sales territory in which a competitor was gaining a foothold. Their job was to "knock out" the competitor using tactics both admirable and questionable. And if his lawyers or the knockers could not eliminate the competition, NCR did what many B2B companies still do today to thwart upstart competitors: It bought them.

The list of important innovations and refinements at NCR has proved to be enduring. If anyone was the designer of the operating blueprint for today's B2B product supplier, we believe it was Patterson. But you may ask how the actions of a single company could possibly have led to a standard for B2B commercial operations more than 125 years later? Partly the answer can be found in the vast amount of writing that was done in those days about NCR's meteoric rise. There were many books and articles written about the company's success and its specific tactics. Patterson himself gave many speeches around the world on NCR business practices. But most scholars agree that it was not what was written or said about NCR that made it so influential; it was the people who worked there.

Many smart people worked and learned under the tutelage and guidance of John H. Patterson at NCR. A shocking number of them would go on to become presidents of many of the most important B2B companies in the United States in the early 20th century, including Burroughs, Standard Register, Toledo Scale, National Automatic Tool, Addressograph-Multigraph, and the research laboratory at General Motors. All would carry their knowledge of NCR's tried-and-true operating models forward and would emulate them at their new companies.

But one top NCR employee might really be the answer to your question. Similar to his contemporaries, he too brought vast numbers of NCR's operating practices to his company when he took over as its new president.

His name was Thomas J. Watson, and the company Watson became president of was the Computing Tabulating Recording

Company, but you may know that company better by its later name, International Business Machines (IBM).

It is believed that much of the construction of IBM's vaunted Blue Suit sales force was based directly on the NCR model. IBM's operating models, in turn, became the standard for an untold number of companies. Many experts argue that under Watson, IBM became not only the most admired company in the B2B world, but also the most copied one. With the large penetration of markets far and wide by IBM and the other companies led by disciples of John Patterson, his thinking spread. Patterson took on the tough challenges of building a successful business out of a complex product. His innovative approaches would then go on to define how many future B2B product suppliers would organize, operate, and grow revenue—in essence, how they would think. Much of that thinking was, and still is, based on a single, overarching objective: how to efficiently transfer the maximum number of product assets from the supplier's balance sheet to the customer's balance sheet.

The B2B Totem Pole

Across many big B2B and business-to-consumer (B2C) companies, both high-tech and near-tech, we see tremendously consistent patterns in how they operate. We see Patterson's fingerprints all over them. The pattern recognition is especially high among B2B companies. Take, for example, strategy decision making. In B2B suppliers today, the chief executive officer (CEO) is obviously the final decision maker. But what really happens is a strategic thought process conducted by a collective "brain" derived from many people on the executive team. However, those people, even if they are all at the same executive level, do not always have the same influence on the collective brain. The people often have a sort of status rank, almost like a totem pole.

The Decision Totem Pole of B2B Suppliers

R&D: Tries to build products that keep sales successful.

Sales: Often drives the company's short- and mid-term thinking.

Services: Tries to profitably deliver what sales sold given the limitations of the product and the customer contract.

Marketing: Generates leads for sales.

FIGURE 1.6 The Decision Totem Pole of B2B Suppliers

In most large high-tech and near-tech B2B companies today, research and development (R&D) and sales own the two top "heads" of the totem pole (see Figure 1.6). Which one is on top and which one is in second position on any given decision is not what is critical. What matters is that, as it was at NCR and at IBM, these same two influencers most often take the lead when B2B companies make critical decisions. At young B2B companies, R&D or engineering executives usually occupy the top spot. Once B2B companies become large, they come to have a huge investment in the sales force or reseller network that they rely on to provide a "return" in the form of revenue and growth. Together, the two influences work to keep sales channels fed with products to sell and keep optimized for coverage and quality. These become the driving considerations of the collective brain of most B2B companies. The two levers of growth are assumed to be adding products and adding salespeople.

By contrast, services and marketing are often seen as important but nonstrategic heads on the totem pole. Service quality is important because it maintains customer satisfaction and it can be a profitable adjunct to the core product business—important roles to be sure, but not strategic. Marketing in B2B companies often finds itself limited to making the sales effort easier, ideally by providing high-quality leads for the sales organization to pursue. Although B2B marketing may once have been the home of strategic planning, marketplace decision making, and business model selection, this is rarely the case today. In most B2B companies we see, those roles are ceded to the top two heads on the totem pole. Services and marketing usually occupy the spaces near the ground, not in the rarified, strategic air of sales and R&D.

A key part of the sales organization's qualification for sitting in one of the top spots has to do with its esteemed position of speaking for the customer's wallet. If you walk into the headquarters of most medium-size or large B2B companies today and scream, "Who owns the customer?" the answer you are most likely to hear echoing through the halls is, "Sales!" That is one of the strongest legacies of men such as Patterson and Watson. They built pioneering, world-class bridges between their companies and their customers, and in most B2B companies, those bridges were—and still are—owned by the sales organization.

Current B2B Favors Suppliers

What has not been written about is the idea that such broad adoption of the NCR/IBM operating model may also have unwittingly established a de facto standard for how business customers expect their suppliers to interact with them. We would assert that B2B supplier practices have been so consistent across so many suppliers for so long that they have conditioned customers to grade them using a scorecard that was, ironically, designed by suppliers. For that reason, the scorecard was designed to favor the supplier's self-interest, not that of the customer. This is a critical point.

Customers accept that their primary bridge to the supplier is going to be through their salesperson (see Figure 1.7). They expect

The Foundations of the Current B2B Model

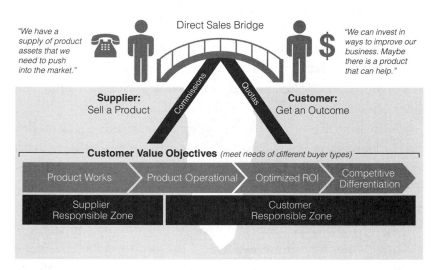

FIGURE 1.7 The Foundations of the Current B2B Model

a lot of attention from that salesperson in the buying process. But they also know that this salesperson is going to be highly motivated by his or her incentive plan to focus on where the next new deal is, not necessarily to hang around and see how they are doing every day. They accept that once the deal is signed they will be seeing . . . well, let's just say somewhat less of their salesperson. They then expect someone in the supplier's service organization, who may or may not actually know what sales promised but who has been assigned the task of getting the product into production, to show up. Although it is not always pretty, ultimately that service person (or team) usually gets the asset up and running. At that point, unless there is a problem with its operation, customers know that the supplier's presence will slowly dwindle. They now own the asset, and the responsibility for turning that operating asset into business value is largely theirs. If customers don't use the product often or well, or if they don't get a return from their investment in that asset, it is really not the fault of the supplier. We would argue that this de facto set of customer expectations is the result of experiencing a highly consistent set of suppliers who all operate pretty much the same way, and have for many decades. There may be variations, and there are certainly exceptions, but we would argue this supplier-customer partnership arrangement is the model most often agreed to either tacitly or formally. It has been a phenomenally widespread approach.

But there are cracks in the foundation of this great model. B2B technology companies are now coming face-to-face with the same dilemma that Patterson did when he bought NCR in 1884. It's our view that, once again, the standard B2B operating model is being overwhelmed by complexity.

As an example, today's suppliers still attempt to employ "canned" product demonstrations presuming that the same demo script about the same offer can be used successfully at prospective customer after prospective customer. But many B2B product companies—especially if they have a significant software component to their product—are seeing their sales costs skyrocket. Technology product complexity, diversity, connectivity, and flexibility have rendered simple sales demonstrations almost obsolete. Instead, teams of experts from the supplier are now assembled and brought in to persuasively and effectively present how the product could best match the unique needs of a particular customer. Salespeople—and often the products themselves—must align vertically within markets, not horizontally across many industries. At other times, impromptu networks of suppliers need to band together in order to form a complete solution to a single customer's complex challenges. And on the customer side, the idea of a single decision maker choosing a technology supplier is becoming increasingly rare. There are financial buying influencers and technical influencers and user influencers and regulatory influencers. There are procurement specialists, lawyers, and risk mitigation experts. And by the time the long and complex sales process has finally neared its end, the customer's business needs may have changed. The increasing complexity of many of today's B2B technology solutions is making many companies on both sides wonder: Is there a better way?

We think one bottom-line observation—unpopular though it may be—needs to be made: The standard B2B operating model was designed to optimize a supplier's "push" of prepackaged products to customers via large, up-front deals. The goal was usually to get the maximum amount of product assets transferred from the supplier's balance sheet to the customer's balance sheet in one big order. But today the assumption that a customer can determine in advance exactly what it needs and then take on all the responsibility for the level of value that it gets from a complex business product is becoming less acceptable. Customers need their suppliers to step up and get into the outcome game. Who owns the asset is not the critical question anymore—in fact, customers often now view owning the asset as a negative.

Again, to be clear, we are not saying that this statement is always true in every customer-supplier partnership. What we are saying is that it is becoming increasingly true in an increasingly large number of them.

A Stairway to Value

We suggest that it is time to upgrade to a more flexible approach on both sides. We need to create a more modern B2B partnering model for high-tech and near-tech industries—one that better mirrors the current complexities and opportunities brought about by software. It should present both sides with a clear understanding of who does what and what value should be expected. It should be flexible enough to work well at different levels of solution complexity. Each step could be chosen as a permanent model for partnering, or it could evolve as the partnership becomes more complex and strategic over time.

Let's face it: Not all B2B products are the same. Some are simple and some are not. Some are well understood by the customer's employees, and some are not. Others are easy to use at first, but become more complicated as the customer tries to use it more aggressively. Some products "just run," whereas others need much more ongoing management and optimization. The bottom line is that business customers need different levels of supplier partnerships for different purposes. What we need is a new partnering model that offers a stairway to value (see Figure 1.8).

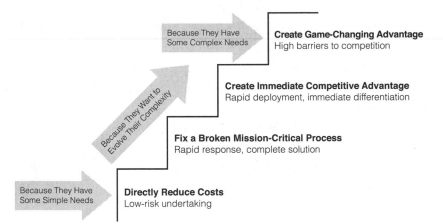

Customers Want a Stairway to Value

FIGURE 1.8 Customers Want a Stairway to Value

The partnering model for a relatively simple B2B product offer is well understood. It is exactly what NCR designed and built and is the B2B standard with which we are all familiar. In choosing a supplier for such a partnership, customers already know all the important questions to ask:

- Is the supplier credible?
- Do I trust the salesperson?
- Does the product function adequately?
- Is it materially better than my in-house options?

- How competitive is the price?
- Is the product reliable?
- Are the warranty length and service offers acceptable?
- What are the financing options?
- Can we/they get it installed and running?
- Will it work with all the other stuff we already bought?

Experienced corporate buyers developed basic supplier selection criteria such as these over years and years of purchasing capital equipment. Customers who are versed in owning and operating particular product types can rely on their experience and judgment to sift through the answers from multiple bidders to questions such as these and arrive at the supplier choice that is best for them. And perhaps more important, they know they can rely on their experience and the knowledge of their internal staff to extract value from the assets once they own them. For these deal types, placing a large, up-front purchase in exchange for the lowest possible price makes perfect sense.

In 2009, one of the authors published a book titled *Complexity Avalanche*.[11] In that book he drew a very simple picture that became widely circulated in the tech industry. We call it the "consumption gap" (see Figure 1.9). The notion is one that nearly everyone can identify with either as a businessperson or as a consumer.

The Consumption Gap

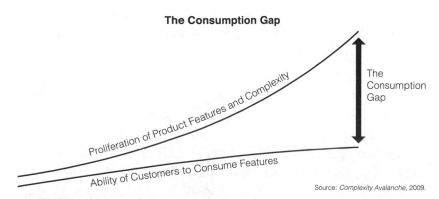

Source: *Complexity Avalanche*, 2009.

FIGURE 1.9 The Growing Consumption Gap

Tech companies, especially those whose products have a considerable software component to them, make every possible effort to differentiate their product by adding features. They add features, and they add features, and they add features. They have legions of talented engineers, scientists, and software developers. These people are measured and incentivized by making the supplier's products more feature-rich. From the manufacturer's perspective, the shift to software is great news. Once a software component is added to a product, companies can create new and amazing features faster and cheaper than in practically any other form of product development: no factories to build, no dies to cast, and no natural resources to deplete. From that day, you can count on a rapid proliferation in the features and capabilities of that product. First, it's just some basic features. Soon new features will be built on top of the last ones, and so on, and so on.

The good news is that more features means that the potential value of business technology products will increase every day. The return on investment (ROI) that they *could* deliver and the outcomes that they *could* provide grow at an increasing rate. The bad news is that much of that increased value is trapped beyond the reach of many business customers. They may not have the time, the skills, and/or the quantity of labor to fully implement the full potential of the products they purchase. Businesses today are not trying to increase the number of employees in areas such as IT or operations; they are trying to reduce them. CEOs and chief financial officers (CFOs) are actively pressing chief information officers (CIOs) and production executives to improve the return on their technology investments, and often that means reducing the costs of expensive internal resources. At most companies today, the ability to consume complexity is not going up; it is intentionally being driven down.

Let's look at one of today's hottest B2B investment areas to illustrate the case. There is a lot of talk today about the value of big data and analytics. Many businesses are investing in technology and software to make their operations smarter. But according to a recent survey,[12] 57% of finance executives say that their companies are "fair" or "poor" at ensuring big data and similar IT projects yield expected returns. More than two-thirds give their companies a "C" or "D" in even being able to measure the returns.[13] Why are the scores so bad? Simple—because producing returns is complicated. It is probably not because these companies did not buy the right hardware or software products from their suppliers. It is probably not because those products were not installed properly. It is probably not because the suppliers were not available to fix problems if they developed. In short, it is not because the supplier did not deliver its part of the contractual partnerships. It is because owning technology products is one thing. Getting these products to deliver on their potential—to make them deliver real ROI—is another (see Figure 1.10).

The growing number of complex B2B product offers is laying bare a structural weakness in the standard B2B customer-supplier partnering model that worked so well for so long. The

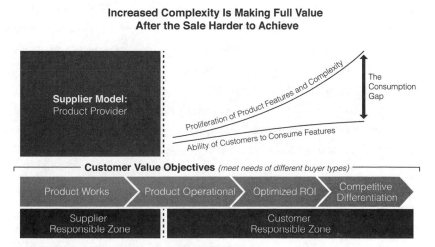

FIGURE 1.10 Increased Complexity Is Making Full Value After the Sale Harder to Achieve

consumption gap is rendering obsolete the notion that the customer alone should be responsible for the outcome it gets from a product. As a result, too many business investments either never break even or produce an ROI that is too low or too difficult to identify and impossible to prove. Some CIOs are being saddled with reputations of being bigger contributors to overhead than they are to revenue and profits. Employee end users get frustrated trying to use products that simply do not work the way they need to. This often has a negative effect on productivity and morale. And in perhaps the most insidiously persistent sting of this phenomenon, the technology products—once implemented—cannot be withdrawn. As we pointed out, components rarely stay components. They are integrated into something larger. That larger thing might be mission critical to the customer. That larger thing is not easy to do without. That larger thing is costly to have in an inoperable state. In short, once the customer "goes live" with the new product, they are usually committed to it—high ROI or not.

That is *great* news for the supplier in the current B2B model. The cost for the customer to rip and replace its product becomes prohibitive. That means the customer is committed to paying for product maintenance, parts, upgrades, and add-ons. However, that is *not* great news for the customer. The story in the IT industry is very well known. It is generally accepted that 80% of a business customer's corporate IT budget goes not to adding more innovative capability, but to the maintenance and management of the current systems. Is that really the best use of the company's capital? No right-thinking businessperson would answer yes to that question. But that is the by-product of taking an old partnership model—one built for a time of simpler products—and pulling it forward into the age of complexity.

Why have suppliers not been motivated to solve this growing customer consumption gap? It can largely be explained by the economics that lie at the heart of the traditional B2B product sale. You see, most business customers agree to pay up front for the products and services they buy (see Figure 1.11).

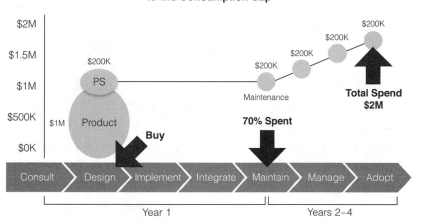

FIGURE 1.11 The Old Model Often Made Suppliers Insensitive to the Consumption Gap

Let's take this example from the current B2B, capital expenditure (CapEx) partnering model. In Figure 1.11, a customer is spending $2 million over four years for a technology supplier's products and services. The arrows at the bottom of the figure illustrate where in the ownership-cycle timeline the customer pays the supplier. In the vast majority of B2B capital equipment transactions, the customer pays for the product and installation services once they are delivered. Usually, the customer also purchases a maintenance contract from the supplier that begins once the warranty period expires. In our example, that is 20% per year. This means that at the end of the first year of ownership, 70% of the entire $2 million that the customer will spend is already transferred to the supplier. The last 30% comes in ratably over the remaining three years from the maintenance contract. We know from our research at the Technology Services Industry Association (TSIA) that the likelihood of that maintenance revenue being captured by the supplier is very high. Renewal rates for maintenance contracts can range from 70% to nearly 100%, depending on the product category.

What all this means is that until now, what "rang the bell" for a supplier was the signing of the contract. This one event locked in lots of up-front revenue and profit. Some suppliers muted the customer impact through leasing or guaranteed subscriptions, but still, the customer was fully committed once the contract was executed. After that, the supplier's risks were minimal and the cash-flow profile was excellent. The supplier's lever to optimize the profitability of the deal after that was to minimize the variable costs of delivery—to *not* become involved more than the maintenance contract's service-level agreements (SLAs) required.

Customers, on the other hand, had the exact opposite scenario. Their financial benefit came only after the business problem had been addressed and its profitability had increased. This may have come as soon as the new products were turned on. But in many cases, realizing that return took months or years due to complexity. They were committed to paying the supplier for its products and services, but the consumption gap often meant that extracting true value was far less than a sure thing. The cold-hard fact is that, for the longest time, the risk-and-reward profile in the traditional B2B model was out of alignment (see Figure 1.12).

Risk and Reward Were Misaligned

Economic Value to the Customer

Economic Value to the Tech Company

Financial Gain

Length of Product Ownership

Source: *Consumption Economics*, 2011.

FIGURE 1.12 The Traditional B2B Model: Misaligned Risks and Rewards

The financial value of the partnership to the supplier was highest at the front end, and the value to the customer was highest sometime out in the future—that is, assuming they were successful at overcoming the consumption gap.

This is where you see, on a grand scale, the negative effect of dragging Mr. Patterson's 125-year-old business model design into the age of complexity. The customer value left on the table by a B2B operating model designed simply to optimize asset transfer is incalculable. It's not that suppliers are evil; this is simply how they optimize the profitability of their deals. They are optimizing for shareholders, not for customers. And yet through decades of conditioning, customers have willingly come to accept this model.

Years of running this complexity playbook has resulted in an "excess inventory" situation, but not the one normally associated with that term. In the traditional world of tangible products, we think of excess inventory as inventory that is sitting in our manufacturing plants or in the warehouses of our channel partners. In a software-eaten world, the excess inventory is made up of product capability that is bought, installed, and available for use within the customer's organization, but is either underutilized or—in the worst cases—not utilized at all. Because the incentives of Patterson's B2B model are a lot more push than pull, customers are stuffed to the gills with excess capability. This represents a massive overhang on their future purchases of the next generation of solutions.

So what kinds of activities could eliminate or substantially reduce the risk for the customer in getting faster and better returns from complex technology? Here are, as examples, three areas that we believe could radically reduce the pain:

- **Radical reduction in "overhead complexity."** This means building technology products that are much easier to install, configure, tailor, integrate, and upgrade. The time and money a customer spends on these tasks are pure overhead. They create absolutely no value or return for the customer.

- **Remote supplier management.** What if the customer did not have to rely on internal staff to manage the product's day-to-day performance? We are in the age of the Internet, right? Why can't suppliers better manage their products for customers on a one-to-many basis?

- **Feature control.** What if end-business users only saw the features they really needed to use, and not all 5,000 that exist in the product? What if the feature set's complexity unfolded to them as their mastery of the basics became evident? What if they unfolded intelligently based on an individual's specific job role and in the order that upper management felt was most advantageous to the business?

There are many other things that could be added to the list of barriers to complexity adoption in a B2B context. But it's hard to argue that these three things aren't great examples of items that could materially help drive more rapid and more successful utilization of complex technology products. So why aren't they being done? Why does complexity still rain heavily on a technology business solution's ROI parade?

The answer, ironically, is simple and is a main point of this book. Customers are still accepting tasks in the partnership that really should belong to the supplier. We would submit that not one of these three things would be best accomplished from the customer side. Yet, customers soldier on. They hire systems integrators to deal with the overhead complexity that the supplier failed to engineer out of the product. They add employees who become its system administrators. They hold back from deploying entire modules or components because many of the employee end users are not ready for it.

The idea that these responsibilities are best suited to the customer in the partnership is just plain crazy. It simply doesn't work anymore. Let's face it: The simple "one size fits all" B2B model is dead or dying at various rates of speed. In enterprise high-tech, we would already say RIP. In other near-tech B2B sectors, the signs may not be as evident but the symptoms are worsening. Just take your own company's temperature. Feel it?

Suppliers Get into the Game

But now, something is changing—at least in the world of B2B high-tech. New pricing models are taking the industry by storm, as shown in Figure 1.13.

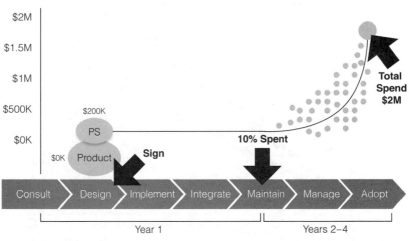

FIGURE 1.13 New, Rapidly Emerging "Anything-as-a-Service" (Operational Expenditure) Purchase Patterns

They have different names, such as software as a service (SaaS) or managed services, and different forms, such as pay-per-user, pay-per-transaction, or pay-per-unit rates (the little dots in Figure 1.13), but they all have one thing in common: The customer only pays for what they consume. There is even talk about revenue-sharing or gain-sharing arrangements. These pricing models mean that the customer pays much less up front—sometimes nothing at all. The supplier only gets to bill the customer when the customer utilizes the product. This shift away from purchasing with capital equipment budget dollars in favor of purchasing "by the drink" using operating budgets is shocking in its speed and pervasiveness. It changes the entire deal profitability profile for a supplier. Rather than being profitable from the moment the product is delivered to the customer, suppliers might not realize profitability on a deal for months or years. Thousands of suppliers are now facing the same risk-and-reward profile that their customers are (see Figure 1.14).

XaaS Drives True Risk/Reward Alignment

Economic Value to the Tech Company

Economic Value to the Customer

Financial Gain

Length of Product Ownership

Source: *Consumption Economics,* 2011.

FIGURE 1.14 How "Anything as a Service" (XaaS) Drives True Risk/Reward Alignment

At that point, something magical happens. A switch is flipped in the collective strategy brain of the supplier. The consumption gap is no longer a theoretical problem shouldered by customers. The consumption gap is now a direct threat to the supplier's revenue and profit. The totem pole begins to ask itself new questions, to reconsider what is strategic. The result is that maybe for the first time in more than 125 years, both parties in the B2B partnership are open to a new model—a model in which the supplier is involved in the success of its customers permanently and in real time.

This opening chapter started with one key premise: The operating model used by business technology suppliers is about to be revolutionized. After a long and successful run, "B2B 1.0" looks antiquated. We have simply gone too long without any real innovation in terms of the agreements and roles that underpin the B2B economy—especially in the high-tech and the exploding number of near-tech industries. The increasing complexity quotient of products is the straw that finally broke the camel's back.

Customers are looking for new ways to achieve business value with their strategic partners. But how would these new models work? What would they look like? What is *really* about to happen to B2B?

2 | New Leaders Emerge

N<small>OT SURPRISINGLY, THE TWO PARTIES IN A B2B PARTNERSHIP</small> are not the only ones with a natural divide between their fundamental self-interests. B2C companies also wake up each day thinking about how to push their supply of product assets into the arms of prospective consumers (see Figure 2.1). Consumers, on the other hand, usually only consider involving these companies in their lives if they think these companies will give them an experience they really want or need.

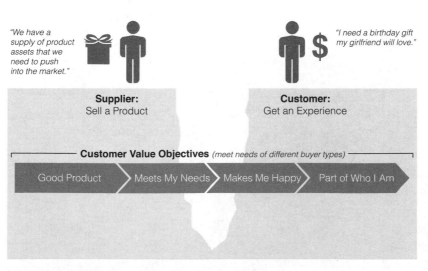

FIGURE 2.1 B2C Companies Also Face a Divide

Although it's a similar challenge, important differences face B2C suppliers. Take the outcome: Usually business customers are seeking quantifiable financial outcomes—more revenue, lower cost, higher customer satisfaction. Consumers often seek an experience as their goal. It could be the experience of looking good by wearing trendy clothes at a cheap price. It could be having fun with great video games. Or it could be feeling good by owning a product whose brand makes a statement about who they are as a person. Their value objectives can be somewhat different, less empirical. A second difference is often the breadth and depth of consumer choice. There aren't just a few clothing manufacturers to choose from; there are thousands. There aren't just a few car manufacturers; there are dozens. The same holds true with cameras, phones, and watches. This also weighs heavily on the minds of B2C suppliers. How do they stand out in a vast sea of competition waiting to deliver a similar experience to a particular consumer?

But perhaps the biggest difference is simply price. Most often, the average price of a consumer sales transaction is a tiny fraction of a B2B sales transaction. Sure there are a few consumers who could buy a $200,000 watch, but not many. There are a lot more Casios sold than there are Patek Philippes. Even when a consumer pays the same price for a product as a business does, they buy far fewer units at a time. When a consumer buys a new multifunction printer for their home, they buy *one* multifunction printer. A business might buy 10, 100, or a 1,000. Thus, lower prices and small unit volumes force product manufacturers in the B2C world to focus heavily on the cost and efficiency of their distribution, delivery, and service—basically, how they design their operating models.

Do you remember the 1980s? At that time, B2C companies looked up to B2B companies.

B2B companies were considered the big, global power players. They had sophisticated sales forces and huge direct service organizations. Sure, Apple was cool and Microsoft was profitable, but they were pioneering engineers of a hot new technology.

There was not very much that was cool or innovative about their distribution model. It was classic B2C of its day. They used independent retailers to sell their consumer technology in the same way that clothing manufacturers sold through department stores and refrigerator makers sold through appliance stores. What choice did they have? They couldn't afford to hire an expensive direct sales force to sell to consumers. They had to rely on independent reps, just like B2B companies did before John Patterson came along. And they suffered from the same problems that Patterson knew he had to avoid. B2C companies had little real control of the quality of their distribution or their service. They didn't know if the dealer's salespeople knew what they were talking about or if they were going to recommend their product or a competitor's. They also had no idea whether the dealer was going to help the customer get the product working or not. And if the customer had a problem, the product company could do little but hope that the dealer was going to fix it in a satisfactory way.

Back then, many B2C product companies had virtually no control over their end customer's ownership experience. Many of them wanted no part of it! The low prices of their products and the way they thought about their operating models led them to conclude that touching the end consumer was not just impractical; it would be a financial disaster.

And then in 1995, software and the Internet began to eat B2C.

What started as an interesting way to sell books triggered a chain of events that revolutionized the world of commerce. Amazon was not the first company to actually sell products over the Internet, but it sure as heck popularized it. Far more important, it made a science out of it. There were lots of raised eyebrows at B2C companies as the sales numbers for leading Internet retailers started to roll in. These weren't little sales numbers; they were in the billions. Everyone quickly got the message and started investigating what it would take for them to sell direct. It might have been that their primary goal was simply to supplement revenues by adding a direct channel to their traditional indirect ones. Or it could be that they were actively investigating whether they could disintermediate their channel, all or in part. Either way, it quickly caught on.

But the early days of e-commerce were not what they are today. There were websites that looked like they had taken a photo of their paper brochure and added a toll-free 800 number at the bottom. That wasn't really innovative; it didn't even really attempt to sell. It was just primitive online advertising. But the big boys of online retail saw the opportunity differently. Pioneers such as Amazon, eBay, and Dell were thinking a different, more radical thought: How can we conduct a successful, positive, and *complete* sales cycle over the Internet?

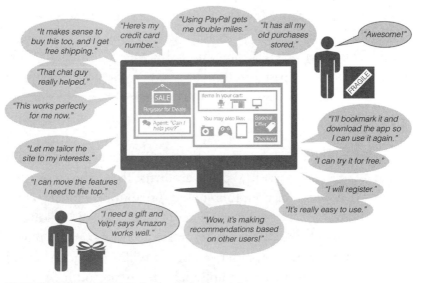

FIGURE 2.2 The B2C E-Commerce Innovation

By starting modestly, selling simple items, the true B2C e-commerce innovators turned art into science (see Figure 2.2). You probably could have taken a survey of 1,000 salespeople at retail stores in 1995 when Amazon started its service, and not one of them would have said that a machine could do their job. Selling was art.

They wouldn't have been totally wrong, but they certainly weren't right. Online retail sales grew quickly. From nearly nothing in 1995, sales passed $100 billion just a decade later. They are now over $200 billion, and Forrester is predicting $370 billion by 2017.[1] That's just in the United States. Globally it will soon be nearing $1 trillion—amazing!

The growing science behind today's e-commerce is equally amazing. Although not perfect, it has proven itself enough to change the way both B2C companies and their consumer customers operate forever. For thousands of years, consumers bought clothes, furniture, books, wine, jewelry, and pets from people. Now, millions of them buy every day from a machine.

The Supplier Side

How did this happen? How did face-to-face sales and service, two of the oldest commercial professions, start getting elbowed out of the B2C distribution equation so quickly? Well, as it turns out, another guy from the past—in this case, way in the past—may give us the most succinct answer. It was Plato, in 369 BC, who supposedly first wrote the phrase, "…and yet the true creator is necessity, who is the mother of our invention."

As we pointed out, most non-luxury B2C companies rely on selling a high volume of low-price products. To do this, most utilized a two-, three-, or even four-tiered distribution model so that they could eventually get a human being (a salesperson) talking to another human being (a consumer) at the point of sale in a physical location where a consumer would be willing to go. At every tier, they sacrificed margin points. Take the wine business as an example. Wineries usually had to offer a hugely discounted price (more than 50% off retail) to the distributor (who keeps 20%), who was offering a healthy discount to the retailer (who keeps

20%), who was offering wine to the consumer "at a great 10% discount." Multitiered consumer distribution models have been around for years. At each tier, they eat into the original product company's revenue and margin. Is it any wonder that when an alternative distribution model came along that had the potential to eliminate tiers (with their demanding discounts), the product manufacturers pounced? Is it also any wonder why everyone in the downstream part of the distribution chain then became nervous? But it's ironic that the ones who were the true pioneers were not the original equipment/product manufacturers. Amazon doesn't make anything; it is a distributor of other manufacturers' products. But Amazon saw the business model advantage of cutting out just one or two tiers while offering the consumer a wide selection of products and a great price. Software and the Internet created an online shopping experience that disintermediated retail stores and physical salespeople.

For purposes of our conversation about B2Bs, the important question is not why they did it, but how. At a very high level, the answer is that some teams of smart people began dissecting the art of selling and servicing. Although we are sure they absolutely saw art in selling, they wanted to know where and when and why art was required. They wanted to understand how and what kind of advice was expected from the salesperson. They wanted to know how much advice consumers got from information sources other than the salesperson—such as comments from their friends or what they read in a magazine. They wanted to know what held them back from actually buying when they saw something they liked. They wanted to figure out how to incent people who were close to buying to actually buy—maybe by allowing them to customize the offer until it was "just right." They wanted to know how to take some risk out of the purchase, to give the consumer the confidence to hit that BUY button. They endeavored to create an experience whereby the consumer could be confident that they'd be really happy—or if in the rare case they weren't, they'd be taken care of immediately and cheerfully. And lastly, they wanted to figure out how to get those people to come back for that experience over and over and over.

In the same way that scientists cure intractable diseases and NASA put a man on the moon, Amazon became the $60 billion juggernaut it is by assigning smart people to the task of building a great online experience. The company armed these people with modern tools and instructed them to go do research about why customers buy and how they consume.

The B2C Totem Pole

Modern B2C companies have learned to think differently. They have formed a different strategic totem pole, as shown in Figure 2.3.

The Decision Totem Pole of B2C Suppliers

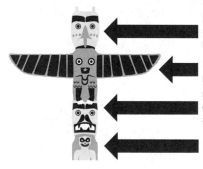

Marketing: Owns customer and market understanding. Offers customer experience and platform planning. Drives reputation and trial.

Development: Tries to build an innovative platform within Marketing's parameters.

Services: Operates the platform, owns the customer relationship. Drives utilization and sales volume.

Sales: Generates leads for services.

FIGURE 2.3 The B2C Totem Pole

In the modern B2C world, marketing could be referred to as "Big M Marketing": not just lead generators for the sales force, as it often is in B2B, but also what it was in the greatest moments of P&G—one of the top heads in the company's collective strategy brain. Whether any individual company refers to that planning function as "marketing" is not the point. What matters is that the collective brain of the company focuses obsessively on understanding the customer, and then on applying development resources to the "white spaces" revealed by that understanding. Every B2B company says it does that, but few really do it. In the modern B2C world, the bridge that spans suppliers and consumers operates wholly differently from most B2B companies. At many high-tech and near-tech B2B companies, R&D builds what it thinks is exciting, and sales is tasked with selling it. For many of them, it has been an incredibly successful model. But that is not how the modern B2C totem pole normally operates.

A Platform of Service

There is another sea change of huge significance that has rarely been discussed. Like B2B companies today, few B2C companies back in the mid-1990s saw service quality as a path to real shareholder value. To them, it was just a set of costs to be tightly managed in a low-margin, high-volume business. At that time, it would have been a correct conclusion. Customer service technology was pretty primitive. Providing good customer service was an equation that involved applying labor—the kind personified by the Maytag repairman on US television in the 1970s and 1980s. Because of its high labor cost, few consumer product companies were known for great customer service. It was sporadic, and usually dependent on heroic activities far down in the distribution chain, such as a local dealer who believed sincerely in the power of good service.

To most B2C companies of the 1990s—and to many B2B companies today—sales and service were truly bifurcated thoughts. In their collective brain, the "sales motion" was separate from the "service motion." They viewed the two motions as different kinds of people, with different skill sets doing different kinds of things at different points for different reasons. And certainly they prioritized the sales motion. Like Patterson's B2B model, the operating model of B2C product companies prior to

1995 was still built to ensure a person-to-person sales motion, albeit far down in the distribution chain.

But today's B2C leaders have a different view. They are building a platform. That platform is designed to create a complete experience—a service—that the consumer will enjoy. It is that platform, that complete service experience, that will sell products. The bridge they build to span their divergent interests with customers is not a sales-force bridge. Instead, progressive B2C companies span the divide between their self-interest and that of the consumer with a bridge designed by marketing. The organization that operates the bridge is customer service. The bridge itself is constructed of technology. And although Patterson's bridge was (metaphorically) "held up" by the two towers of commissions and quotas, the state-of-the-art B2C bridge is held up by the power of data and analytics (see Figure 2.4).

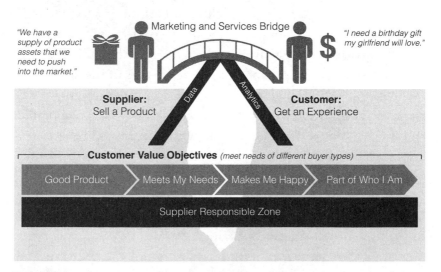

FIGURE 2.4 The B2C Bridge Operates Differently

It is designed from the outset to deliver the full outcome, not just to get the deal. In B2C, one deal is nothing. You don't focus just on selling one deal; you focus on growing a relationship over time. You don't just get the sale, get the money, and *get out*. This is why CEO Jeff Bezos gave Amazon the mission to "be Earth's most customer-centric company." He knows that the platform he designs and the service experience it creates are going to determine how much he sells. He doesn't rely on salespeople to get big deals done; he just wants consumers to try the Amazon experience. That doesn't take a big, expensive sales force. It's the same with Apple. Yes, it has retail stores with salespeople, but its most critical mission is not just to see how big an order it can sell; it is to get people onto critical Apple platforms such as iTunes or the App Store. The salespeople are lead generators for the service experience. That is where they will drive the revenue growth and the profits. The entry point to the platform can be anything—a $3,000 MacBook or a $65 Nano. Either way, the Apple platform will do the selling. Once you're onboard, chances are good that Apple will expand its share of your tech wallet no matter what the entry point was.

B2C companies have done something truly remarkable in the last decade. They have moved from laggards to leaders in the world of business. It is amazing what you can achieve when you have no choice. Necessity—in this case, for a lower-cost sales model that offered higher gross margins—has truly been the mother of invention. If Amazon did not get good at this, it was dead. If tech companies such as Dell and Intuit didn't figure out how to get orders done over the Internet, they would not be nearly as profitable today. To succeed, each had to learn to model and automate a complex customer interaction. That meant they not only had to bring data and analytics to the marketing and sales tasks, but they also had to enable customers to configure custom products, to ensure they are delivered on time, or to deploy and operate them. In addition, B2C companies had to learn to monitor, support, and grow the activity of customers—sometimes millions of them.

They have jumped on an opportunity presented by software and the Internet, and by asking tough questions, they managed to translate the art of selling, executing transactions, satisfying customers, and gaining market share from a human-driven set of activities to a software-driven one. They have built a next-generation supplier model—one that is forcing even the very best operators to fundamentally rethink their businesses. In books, the dramatic reversal of fortune for Barnes & Noble and Borders is well known. In video, Blockbuster is in bankruptcy at the hands of Netflix in spite of a powerful brand and a broad market reach. In electronics, Circuit City went away completely, and Best Buy has been through multiple rounds of restructuring. Adding insult to injury, Amazon has even found a way to reach into the physical store shopping experience of its brick-and-mortar competitors. Powered by Amazon's mobile phone app and its integrated barcode recognition, the price of any product on the floor of any brick-and-mortar retailer can be checked against the exact same product available online. The combination of the mobile revolution and the new B2C model has unwittingly turned these retailers into showrooms for Amazon and other online retailers. The new selling motion for more expensive consumer goods has become "narrow the choice set through online reviews, go touch and feel the product in a retail store, place the order online from your mobile phone for 20% to 50% less, and have the product delivered to your home two days later." The worst part? Traditional retailers have no answers today for how to compete with the power of this new sales motion.

The Customer Side

That's how suppliers have changed in B2C. But as we assert throughout this book, to take full advantage of the remarkable new capabilities of emerging supplier operating models, customers have to change too. And consumers have once again led the way.

Just think about all the changes in consumer behavior that have been achieved in just 15 years! B2C companies have gotten millions of consumers to agree to:

- do business with a supplier where they have never met one single human representative of that company.

- accept that the opinions and behaviors of totally anonymous people should direct their buying decisions in the form of online recommendations and reviews.

- learn—and this is a *big* one—to trust online B2C companies with personal and financial information that they never would have considered giving to someone or some company that they didn't personally know.

- start turning over tasks to suppliers that—for centuries—they assumed they must do themselves, even though they didn't really want to or weren't good at them. Maybe it was letting Bank of America pay their bills automatically every month or using FTD.com to remind them about Mom's birthday. Soon they may rely on an online service from GE Healthcare to tell the doctor how they feel since last week's little medical procedure.

These are just the tip of the iceberg in the huge behavioral and attitudinal changes consumers have made in order to capitalize on the potential of a next-generation operating model offered by progressive suppliers. In our view, these bear an uncanny resemblance to some of the behavioral changes that we see coming for business customers.

Maybe You Disagree

If you are reading this and you are in B2B and you are deep into complexity, you are currently thinking that what we're implying is naive BS. You are thinking that what has been accomplished in B2C could never be replicated in a B2B market space such as yours. "Too complex," you say.

Maybe.

But consider what FedEx has done. On FedEx.com, business customers using their Critical Inventory Logistics Solutions can set up an account, check rates, stock inventory in global warehouses, order pickups, prepare shipping documents, complete customs forms, meet complex international freight regulations, track shipments, pay bills, and run reports on all their activity. Corporate customers literally can manage a global logistics operation on FedEx's website. They can do that from their laptop or their smartphone. If they need help, they can chat, watch a video, or ask someone to call them. FedEx.com hasn't built its website just for lead generation. It is a website built so business customers can manage complete business operations—in this case, for product delivery or parts logistics—all over the world.

What about the transformation going on at Intuit? They are not just selling software online to consumers for their taxes. They are allowing small and medium-sized businesses (SMBs) to manage their entire accounting process over the Internet by turning QuickBooks into a completely online experience. Intuit sees the cloud as a powerfully better way to aggregate customers and to deliver value for them. Today, Intuit has well over a million small business customers doing their accounting and payroll online.[2]

And don't forget about Rackspace. At Rackspace.com, business customers can analyze, price, provision, manage, and secure their business data into the cloud. It has built a bridge to its customers that depends on marketing and service, just like B2C companies. It advertises heavily in airports, business magazines, and even on the radio. Its goal? To get businesses to the cloud-based service platform. Once there, the "Fanatical Support" team at Rackspace takes over. Sure, Rackspace would love to get a huge up-front order. But that is not what it is betting on. It's betting on the idea that once it "lands" you for a trial, it will "expand" you into a big customer.

We think the pattern is clear: B2C innovations are eating their way into the domain of B2B operating models, even in markets once considered to be complex such as enterprise data storage and business software. Putting a huge exclamation point on all this is the unbelievable growth story known as Amazon Web Services (AWS). AWS now offers incredibly complex computing services through the cloud—not just storage or computing power, but also many kinds of technology, including database solutions from Oracle, Microsoft, and SAP, as services. Many venture-funded SaaS start-ups are being counseled to not build a data center at all! This is how complete and powerful the AWS offer is. Yet it retains many unique and powerful consumer-offering attributes. For example, in January 2013, Amazon launched the beta version of what it calls Trusted Advisor. It is an algorithm that automatically compares the actual usage of Amazon's hosting services with the price plan that every AWS customer is on. If it finds that a given customer is on the wrong plan, it automatically notifies him or her with no human interaction. It suggests the price plan that the person should be on to give him or her maximum performance at the lowest cost. Now you could say that decreases Amazon's revenues. It does in the short term. But it does something much more powerful in the medium term. It completely de-risks the purchase decision for customers trying AWS for the first time. They can just pick a price plan that is close and trust that Amazon will help them get on the plan that delivers them the most value based on how they actually use it, not how they think they might use it. How many B2B suppliers today have the sophistication or the perspective necessary to deliver a service to their business customers on terms such as that?

The last intellectual hurdle that B2B executives may need to clear on this topic is the argument that the new model B2B pioneers are not profitable. OK, fair enough. With the exception of Rackspace, they aren't. But we believe that Jeff Bezos at

Amazon and Marc Benioff at salesforce.com—the two companies most often cited in this profit debate—could pretty successfully defend their logic. For them, it's a landgrab. The land in this case is product markets and customers. Both are investing heavily to own as much of that land as they can before someone with an even better operating model stops them. In salesforce.com's case, it is moving across the enterprise software application horizon from sales apps to customer service apps to marketing apps. In Amazon's case, it is moving across what seems to be the entire spectrum of consumer products and now into enterprise IT. That is rightly making a lot of high-tech executives very nervous. We call it "Amazonaphobia": the gripping fear that Amazon is going to set up its B2C model in your high-tech B2B market. Could these companies be more profitable immediately if they slowed their investment in grabbing new markets and customers? Absolutely. Is slowing down their land-grabbing ways in order to prove this essential? So far, the stock market says no.

B2C companies innovated because they had to. A few such as Apple and Amazon are now taking their models with them as they begin to invade B2B markets. At the same time they are being mimicked by progressive B2B start-ups who have the freedom to build any new operating model they want. Most are building something far different from Patterson's old model. They are not just offering a product with as-a-service pricing; they are also developing complete, connected customer experience platforms. In the collective brain of their strategy totem pole, the cloud is not just seen as a cheaper way to sell and service, it is an opportunity to get in the game with customers. In ways both exciting and troubling, their existence raises interesting questions for traditional B2B companies. Will they be able to keep up, remain competitive?

There is an interesting management consulting notion around the idea of designing your fiercest competitor.[3] It made us think: What would the fiercest B2B competitor look like today? If you could take the company that is best at one thing and add it to another that is best at a different thing and keep doing that until you had built a sort of corporate Frankenstein, what shape would it take? So we made a list of attributes that we think would make up an ideal company today and captured the brands that came to the top of our minds on each attribute (see Figure 2.5). It was a funny thing.

What Would Your Fiercest Competitor Look Like?

Workday ⟶ Top-Line Growth Rate of 104%

Google ⟶ EBIT of 25%

Amazon ⟶ Marketing and Sales Cost of 3%

Apple ⟶ Brand Loyalty

IBM ⟶ Hunter Sales Force

Wells Fargo ⟶ Cross-Sell Capability

Salesforce.com ⟶ Developer Community

Zynga ⟶ Speed to Market

Amazon ⟶ User Experience

Cleveland Clinic ⟶ Customer Outcomes

American Express ⟶ Customer Service Experience

FIGURE 2.5 What Would Your Fiercest Competitor Look Like?

Of the 11 brands that came to the top of mind, eight were B2C companies. Two were what you might call "new model" B2B companies—both using a SaaS model. Only one was a traditional B2B company. We guess that the proportions would probably have been flipped on their head in 1995—B2B companies would have dominated. We think B2C companies would have been lucky to post one or two entrants. You try it! Which companies go on your list? Is it led by B2B companies or B2C companies?

B2C companies have found better, more efficient ways to become the best supplier match for their consumers. Along the road, they have emerged as leaders in global business innovation. They have made great progress toward turning the customer success process into a data-driven science, not a human-driven art. They have also taught us that the service experience can be the ultimate platform for selling products. In short, they have begun to master the world of micro upsell and cross-sell transactions (the little dots), shown in Figure 2.6.

New XaaS (OpEx) Purchase Patterns Are Rapidly Emerging

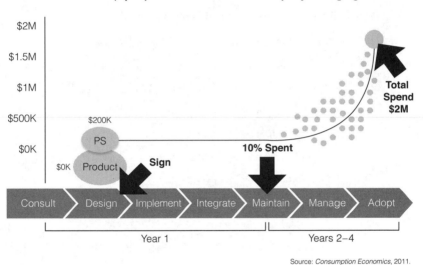

Source: *Consumption Economics*, 2011.

FIGURE 2.6 New Rapidly Emerging Anything-as-a-Service (Operational Expenditure) Patterns

As high-tech and near-tech B2B companies are pulled into consumption-based pricing models by their customers, higher volumes and lower prices will become their norm, too. When it does, the old supplier operating model just won't work anymore. So maybe now, nearly 20 years later, it is time for the teacher to learn a bit from the student.

3 | It's the Outcome!

Every year PricewaterhouseCoopers (PwC) publishes a global CEO survey. In the 2013 edition, 1,330 CEOs gave views on their company's business challenges and prospects for growth. It was an intriguing read. With some facts now on the table about the accuracy of their predictions, it is even more intriguing.

Of CEOs, 80% expected the global economy to stay the same or to decline in 2013. But interestingly, 81% of them were confident in their own growth prospects. At first, that seems like a dichotomy. But then, what else would you have expected? A CEO who is not confident in his or her ability to grow a company—almost regardless of economic conditions—probably should not be its CEO, right? The results for technology company CEOs were no different from the overall group: 76% of them expected the global economy to stay the same or decline while 84% believed their company would grow in the ensuing year.

That's not quite what is happening.

At TSIA we track the financial performance of 50 of the world's largest technology service providers in an index we call the *Service 50*. As you might guess, the vast majority of those large service organizations are embedded within technology product companies such as IBM, SAP, ABB, Fujitsu, and Cisco. In fact, product companies act as host to 8 of the top 10 and 72% of the 50 service organizations. So we closely study their product results, not just their services. The balance of the index is made up of "pure services" companies such as Accenture and Wipro. We think the *Service 50* index is a great proxy for the tech industry over-all because it nicely reflects the blend of business customer tech spending across both products and services.

The *Service 50* data suggests that some tech CEOs may have been a bit too optimistic. In reality, of the large global tech com-panies we track, 56% began 2013 with revenues that stayed flat or shrank from the same quarter the previous year.[1] That is pretty shocking, especially because that trend has been fairly consistent recently. When you look a level deeper, the shock waves get a bit bigger. The vaunted product businesses within these global hardware and software brands took it especially hard—a surpris-ing 66% of them had flat or declining product revenue growth in the first quarter of 2013 compared to the same quarter of 2012. The idea that the famously high-growth, high-tech leaders, as a group, saw their combined revenues shrink 4% is chilling. It would have been worse had not 68% of them been able to grow their services revenue. The continued shift in revenue mix from products to traditional services—a shift that many tech compa-nies don't want to publicly highlight—actually helped mitigate what could have been a much tougher story.

The declining economics of the tech products business is not just a matter of revenue. There is also a margin problem. Hard-ware margins continue to decline almost everywhere. At the same time, sales costs are rising for many reasons. Even large soft-ware companies in the B2B world are struggling to make a profit building and selling new products. Of the 16 software companies in the TSIA *Service 50*, half had flat or declining product busi-nesses. As a group, product revenue for the 16 bellwether soft-ware brands in the *Service 50* shrank 2%. But, like the hardware crowd, 12 were aided on the top line by growing service businesses. As a group, service revenue grew an astonishing 18%.

We don't write press releases on these sobering figures, but the truth is that many companies in the B2B tech industry are struggling just to stay flat. It can't be blamed on the global economy. The world gross domestic product (GDP) for 2013 is predicted to increase 3%.[2] That means that the growth of the combined *Service 50* companies could lag the overall global economy by 7%!

What's more, we fear further bad news is around the corner. We are predicting that the masking effect provided by growing service revenues is not sustainable. We think it's a false positive. The huge majority of these service revenues are what we refer to as "product-attached services": things such as installation and implementation services, customer support, maintenance, and education. For years, supplier service executives were told that they did not need to worry about business strategy because they were safely inside product companies. All the company needed was a good product strategy. Their strong product sales would then pull the services revenue. Except now the product business at many B2B suppliers is shrinking. It is only a matter of time before it pulls the product-attached service business right down with it. That is already starting to happen at some of the biggest tech brands in B2B, and our math suggests it could become widespread within the next few years. When it does, there are going to be many sad faces in Silicon Valley and on Wall Street.

While the facts of recent performance do not seem to have dampened the bullishness of tech CEOs, there is some weakening of the grip. According to the PwC Global CEO Surveys, in 2011, 54% were *very* confident in their annual growth prospects. In 2012, it dropped to 37%; in 2013, to 34%. So the anemic real growth rates at many large tech companies may finally be having an effect on their optimism. We think it's a lot more than just a temporary lull. We think that something pretty fundamental is going on.

Market Maturity

We assert that the old engines on the growth train are running out of steam for many B2B tech suppliers. Although remaining publicly optimistic, many high-tech and near-tech CEOs we talk to sense something is awry. And it is not just the large company CEOs. We have given speeches all over the world since *Consumption Economics*[3] was published, not just to B2B OEMs but also often to their resellers in the channel. They, too, sense that the tech industry is diverging from normal market conditions. Something is definitely amiss.

We think what is amiss has a name, an evil name. It's called market maturity. The consumption gap has finally caught up with an industry that has not had a real revolution in a long time. The "excess capacity" and "good-enough tech" phenomena have fundamentally changed many business customers' buying habits. The appetite for technology asset refresh has slowed in developed countries. Although emerging markets do offer top-line growth, it is growth at the low-end, low-margin range of the product line. Often it is in countries where customers loathe paying for services. Many CEOs privately acknowledge that this won't be enough to carry the day.

Although many in the high-tech arena are busy hyping the cloud right now, the real truth is that the net impact of the cloud will ultimately reduce the amount of hardware, software, and equipment that the business customer has on-site, not increase it. Even when the physical devices are on the customer's premises, such as industrial equipment, the "smarts" will often be in the cloud. High-tech business customers will likely own far fewer assets in far fewer data centers. IT departments or operations staffs will likely be smaller, not bigger. Fewer assets will be customer-owned; more will be supplier-owned and sold on a pay-as-you-go model.

These trends are going to make real growth difficult to come by using traditional approaches. So it's hard to understand why, even in the face of these weak growth numbers and disruptive trends, the tactics that many supplier CEOs plan to utilize to restore growth look so traditional (see Figure 3.1).

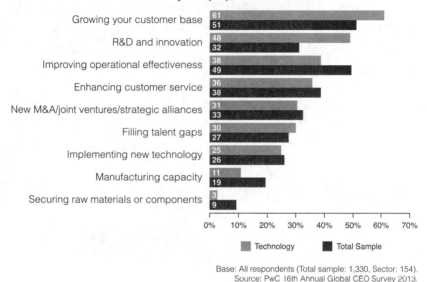

Customer Growth and Investing in R&D and Innovation Remain Top Priorities

Q: What are your top 3 priorities for 2013?

Base: All respondents (Total sample: 1,330, Sector: 154).
Source: PwC 16th Annual Global CEO Survey 2013.

FIGURE 3.1 Top Priorities in Customer Growth and Investing

Everyone is planning to peddle harder—companies are hiring more salespeople, bringing out new products, and trying to adjust pricing schemes, but they can't keep up. It's not that the current operating models of most B2B tech companies are wrong; they just aren't aging well. The collective strategy totem pole at work on the growth problem still seems dominated by the same influences. It's logical to keep doing what had once made your company successful. Suppliers have become used to being in a hot technology market in which each new release puts them back into product-driven hyper-growth. But once the market matures, that play just doesn't work as well anymore. The "more sales reps + more products" engine is suffering major efficiency problems these days. Tech CEOs may be forced to change their game plan. Indeed, 54% of CEOs who responded to the PwC survey said that they are exploring new business models.

But What New Business Model?

That is the key question, the one turning the collective strategy brains at most B2B high-tech and near-tech companies inside out. We have been in the midst of this conversation so many times at so many companies; we think we can boil the quest down to a journey across a simple 2 × 2 matrix, as shown in Figure 3.2.

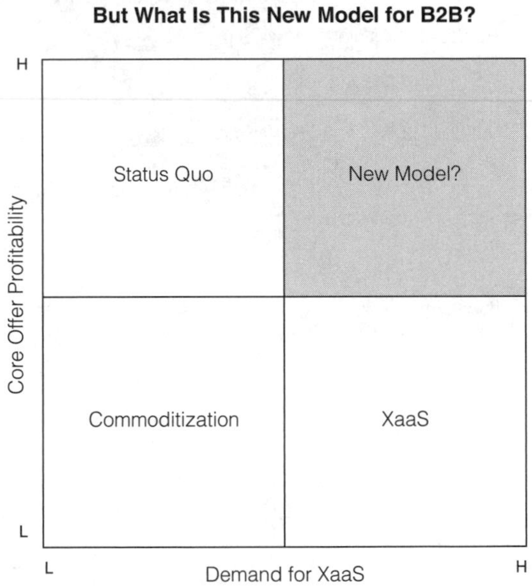

But What Is This New Model for B2B?

FIGURE 3.2   But What Is This New Model for B2B?

Every supplier starts in the upper-left quadrant: business as usual. This means continuing to run the current operating model—probably the one that built the company, the one that the executives understand, that Wall Street knows how to value, that engineers know how to build, and that sales knows how to sell. Frankly, if that model were still a viable growth option, we would not be writing this book and suppliers would not be reading it.

Two macro-market trends are now tempting many high-tech and near-tech product companies to move off that square—to uncomfortably venture out of their comfort zone.

The first trend is growing evidence of deteriorating core-offer profitability. This is what we have highlighted in this chapter: flattening growth, declining margins, increasing sales costs, and traditional service revenues reaching their apex. A couple of years ago, it was easy to blame this on "adverse market conditions," but that excuse is wearing thin. Overall economic growth exceeding the growth of many tech companies is a wake-up call.

The second macro-trend is rapidly growing interest among customers to purchase technology via an "X-as-a-service" model. There are many symptoms of this trend that traditional high-tech suppliers can see and feel. They could be as obvious as XaaS companies that are emerging as competitive threats in new business deals. Or it could be that business buyers are trumping technical buyers in the decision-making process more often. Especially with true cloud architectures, the technical buyers are losing some of their influence. All these are indications of a technology consumption and pricing model that is truly changing. When you can buy jet engines by the hour, computing power by the minute, and computed tomography (CT) brain scans by the image, you know there is demand for XaaS.

This brings us to the question of action. Assuming you are a supplier who is sensing a bit of either commoditization or demand for XaaS (or both), what do you do? That is what the rest of this book is about. Let's start that journey back at our 2 × 2 matrix (see Figure 3.2). The ugliest destination is clearly commoditization. In *Consumption Economics* we talked about what happens at supplier companies when products—even entire product categories—hit (what we termed) the "Margin Wall."[4] The Margin Wall is that horrible place where the cost of developing, manufacturing, and selling a product exceeds the price of the product. Crashing into that wall is no fun for management. It means that there is not

enough value in a product—either organically or competitively—
to support a profitable selling price. If you don't have some profitable downstream offer such as supplies or services, volume won't
help. When whole categories hit the Margin Wall—such as servers
or multi-function printers (MFPs)—even bringing out new products with new features or lower prices won't usually do the trick.
Although they may bring you a few months of profitability, competition quickly catches up, price competition takes over, and the
Margin Wall is soon back in full view.

Commoditization is well known in hardware industries, but
as we have contended (based on our definition, which includes
the cost of manufacturing as well as developing and selling the
product), there are growing numbers of software and software-in-
tensive products that qualify. When a supplier's core offer(s) reach
that point, management's options are limited.

Executives at these companies are not let off the hook by
investors just because they have one or more major product lines
crashing into the Margin Wall. They are still expected to grow and
generate increasing profits. The growth requirement is often met
through increased unit volumes obtained by using price (or low-
end products) to capture market share. The increased profits come
mainly from cutting costs. So although they wait and hope for another hit product, those in management jump from innovation to
cost-reduction as they try to outrun the ugly monster. They spend
all their customer face time talking about their commitment to
R&D and more of their internal time figuring out what jobs they
can eliminate. They know that is not going to be fun. They know
it is not a sign of success. And they know that cutting costs is not
a real business strategy. So, naturally, suppliers go to great lengths
to avoid moving in a straight line from the upper-left quadrant to
the lower-left one, as shown in Figure 3.3.

There have been some interesting efforts to avoid that awful
path. One of the favorite B2B supplier tactics over the last couple
of decades has been to take the commoditized products, mix them

**Many B2B Product Categories Are Commoditizing,
Forcing a Standard Response from Management**

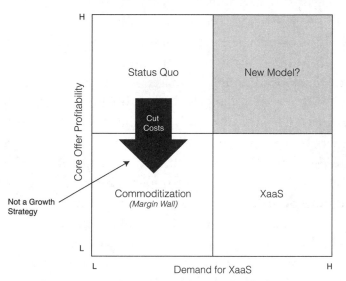

FIGURE 3.3 Many B2B Categories Commoditize, Forcing a Standard
Response from Management

with labor, and bring them to market together as a service. Let's
take a quick look at an important case study—one in which leading suppliers in one of the oldest and most mature segments of
tech made an effort to "fake out" the Margin Wall.

The Lessons of Outsourcing and Early Managed Services

The copier/printer business is huge and has been for decades.
In the glory days of the 1980s and 1990s there were literally
dozens of major manufacturers all around the world who were
high-growth, high-profit, product-driven tech companies. Not
only were the manufacturers profitable but so were their networks of dealers. It was good to be a supplier of office equipment to business customers. Then *crash!* . . . into the Margin Wall
they went. First went the products themselves: Competition
was vast, customers were only using the basic capabilities of the

products, desktop printers were becoming more capable, and prices began to fall. Although not fun, it was survivable. There were still very lucrative aftermarket revenue streams of supplies and service. Toner, paper, and maintenance contracts became the perennial "blades" for the copier/printer "razor." But eventually even that was not enough to maintain the growth and profits demanded by shareholders. So what did many of the market leaders do? They not only provided the devices to their large customers but also offered to supply the labor to optimize and operate them. In one of the earliest, most widespread efforts to outwit commoditization, these suppliers married product with outsourcing. Some called it "outsourcing," whereas others called it "managed services." The basic ones simply offered to take over the job of keeping paper in the trays and toner cartridges full. Why should the customer's employees have to waste their valuable time doing such a thing when the supplier can do it for them using low-priced labor? Other offers aimed squarely at the consumption gap. Suppliers offered to provide staff to operate the customer's in-house copy centers. The value proposition was that the supplier could provide "factory-trained" experts who could operate the sophisticated equipment faster, better, and more efficiently than could the customer's employees. The best suppliers endeavored to study and analyze both the print needs and the print practices of business customers in order to optimize them. Often this analysis could save the customer large amounts of money by optimizing when, where, and on what device documents were produced. Suppliers' logic of marrying labor to the products was that they could sell an outsourcing contract, maybe make a little money on the labor, but far more importantly, the labor "wrapper" would allow them to pull through their product, supplies, and maintenance services at a higher margin. In effect, they used the outsourcing of management or operations to get control of a larger piece of the customer's copy and print spending.

Why is this example so important? Because, although it worked for a period, companies using it ultimately failed to outwit the commoditization monster (see Figure 3.4).

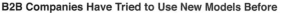

B2B Companies Have Tried to Use New Models Before

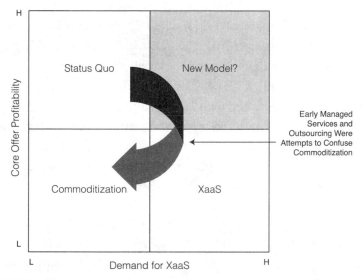

FIGURE 3.4 New Models Tried by B2B Companies

Two things went wrong that offer valuable lessons for tomorrow's successful suppliers. The first was that some suppliers did not focus hard enough on the labor component. They did not innovate ways to eliminate it, and they sometimes allowed themselves to be dragged far out of the domain of their expertise. Because they were either chasing revenue or felt they would lose the print business if they didn't agree, office equipment suppliers started to become office labor suppliers. There were large contracts in which these product companies not only operated their equipment but also ran the mail and drove employee shuttle buses. They allowed themselves to be dragged into areas in which they had no real value, offered no real differentiation, and could capture no real margins. These suppliers were forced far out of their business model and ended up undertaking activities that made no real sense. They ended up adding labor rather than eliminating it.

The second harsh lesson was about pricing in the XaaS world. These managed service contracts were often quite large and complex. They included lots of different devices and software, some in very high quantities. They involved the supplies, often even the paper. They covered the services to install and maintain them and, of course, the labor to operate them. Somewhere along the way, one of the suppliers had a brilliant idea: Let's simplify all this complexity and at the same time take all the risk out of the deal for the customer. How? By taking a multimillion-dollar deal and reducing it to a price per page. It was another first for the industry. Office equipment companies were among the early pioneers of taking large, complex technology solutions and offering them via a true consumption-pricing model. Sure, there was mainframe computing sold by the time slice before this. And there was outsourcing before this. But this was the whole enchilada: the products, the services, the supplies, and the operating labor—at 4 cents per page. The hope was that this approach would not only help simplify things for the customer; it would also be another tool to fake out commoditization. Before per-page pricing, the customer could tell exactly what they were paying for every component in the contract. What were they paying for this device here and for that one over there? How much was the paper? How much was the installation? Armed with that level of pricing, they could pit one potential supplier's bid against all the others at the component level: "Well, your bid is OK on this part, but you need to get a lot more competitive on this other part," they would say. Armed with that visibility, the customer could easily negotiate nearly all the margins out of the whole deal. By bundling it and pricing it by the page, the customer could not see what the component prices were. Early contracts on this pricing model were often very lucrative for the supplier. They applied a data and analytics approach to complex requests for proposals (RFPs) and came up with a pricing model that some competitors were afraid of or took too long to match. It seemed like a brilliant move. They won business and (sometimes) enjoyed solid margins—often much higher than if they had sold just the products alone. It seemed as though they had found a way to successfully confuse the monster.

Until later, that is. You see, by the time those early contracts came up for renegotiation a few years later, the other competitors were no longer afraid of per-page pricing. They too had their big data and analysis spreadsheets. They too could offer the simplicity the customer craved. Not only could they do it, they would do it at 3.8 cents per page.

Well, you can guess what happened next: 3.8 cents became 3.7 cents, which became 3.6 cents. And 15 years later, the price competition hasn't taken a single day off. An early attempt to confuse commoditization actually ended up accelerating it. Because they had not innovated methods to reduce labor or to disengage from the low-value parts while retaining the high-value ones, the gross margins often went down with each successive renegotiation. By bundling a complex solution into a simple, XaaS pricing model these suppliers accidentally drove the entire category down. Consolidation hasn't saved them, offshore manufacturing hasn't saved them, and color hasn't saved them. Today, there is not much money being made by the big office product manufacturers in the business of office products.

The takeaways are clear: First, new models that depend on applying labor to rescue a deteriorating product line are risky business. Second, beware the simple service price list. As far as we can see, every tech category that has adopted this approach has seen a race to the bottom ensue. We would strongly caution against a supplier viewing the switch to a subscription or other consumption-based pricing approach as their "new model." First of all, it's not a new model; it's just a pricing tactic. Second, it is a dangerous one. If they bring the same old supplier operating model and just charge differently for it, they too could face a race to the bottom.

Is XaaS Really the New Model We Seek?

This brings us to the lower-right quadrant. Here we take up the hot B2B debate about the new model du jour—a debate that is raging in the collective strategy brains at many high-tech and near-tech suppliers as well as millions of business customers around the world. The new model du jour is, of course, cloud-enabled XaaS offers. You might call them SaaS; you might call them infrastructure as a service (IaaS) or platform as a service (PaaS). You might call them remote managed services (MS).

That cloud-enabled XaaS is considered the "new model" du jour in high-tech is undeniable. Pick up any business newspaper. Read the tech ads and articles. If they have to do with technology these days, it usually has to do with the cloud. Then insert yourself into an executive meeting at a major tech company. If the members of the executive teams aren't talking cost cutting, they are talking about the cloud, specifically XaaS. Last, grab a seat on your next plane flight right next to a friendly CIO. Should he or she go to the cloud? Shouldn't he or she go to the cloud? Where? When? Why? With whom? Yes, the cloud is big, it's cool, and it's here to stay. There is only one slight problem.

So far, the B2B cloud is unprofitable (see Figure 3.5).

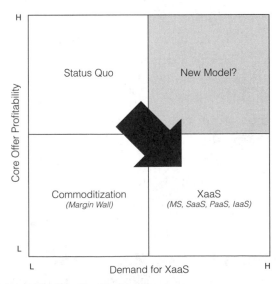

FIGURE 3.5 Current XaaS Is Not Profitable

Technology suppliers, especially those who are feeling the tugs of eroding profitability or slowing growth in their core offers, have to find the explosive growth rates of new XaaS companies such as salesforce.com or AWS awfully compelling. Add to that the increasing customer demand for service-based pricing, asset-less technology, or a less complex ownership experience, and you might wonder why every tech supplier has not moved with great haste from the upper-left to the lower-right quadrant of Figure 3.5. A few have but most have not. Why not? Because they can't.

You have already seen some data from the TSIA *Service 50*. Let us now introduce you to another TSIA tracker we call the TSIA *Cloud 20*. Whereas *Service 50* tracks the largest tech service suppliers, *Cloud 20* tracks many of the largest, most successful XaaS companies. Earlier this year, we debuted a simple chart that compares the average financial performance of companies in the two indexes, shown in Figure 3.6.

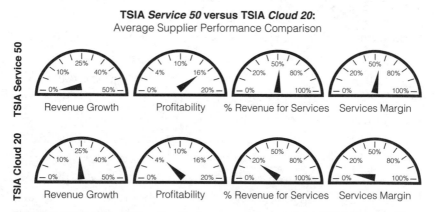

FIGURE 3.6 Average Supplier Performance Comparison: TSIA *Service 50* versus TSIA *Cloud 20*

First, look at the revenue growth of the large, traditional tech leaders that make up the *Service 50*. As we have already discussed, there isn't any. Then contrast that revenue growth with the average growth rate of the companies that make up the *Cloud 20*. Get the picture? Now, look at the profitability comparison. The traditional tech suppliers are still very, very profitable. The profits are under pressure to be sure, and the tactics they are forced to use to deliver those profits are not their preferred ones. But the fact remains: These are profitable companies. Now contrast that with the average profitability of the *Cloud 20* companies at around 4%. That is 75% lower. And there is something behind this data that you can't see. If you tallied just the pure-play B2B XaaS companies, that average profitability drops precipitously. The fact is that of the 20 companies in the index, 11 are unprofitable or barely breakeven. The list of unprofitable B2B SaaS companies includes many of the big brands of the cloud such as salesforce.com, Workday, and NetSuite. Swapping a high-margin business for a breakeven business does not make a lot of sense to investors so far. As traditional tech companies think more deeply about their business model shift, it is not making a lot of sense to them either.

There are two other interesting dials on the dashboard. As we mentioned earlier in this chapter, the revenue and profits from the service businesses at many high-tech and near-tech product companies are the tide keeping the boat afloat at an acceptable level. You get another view of that by looking at the high percentage of total revenue that comes from services among these traditional tech leaders and the high gross margins associated with those offers. Without those contributions, the financial picture looks more than a bit darker. Now contrast that with the XaaS companies. As a group, they look almost like a service-free zone! The percentage of revenue coming from traditional service activities at the average *Cloud 20* company is far less than half that of their traditional counterparts. And rather than being highly profitable, it is a breakeven business.

Is it that there are no services required in the cloud? Generally speaking, no. There are still implementations, integrations, and customer support activities in XaaS offers. In many cases, there may be fewer of them, but not few enough to explain this. So why then? It's because the *Cloud 20* consists of growth companies in land-grab mode. They value new contracts more than profits right now. They love to sell against companies that require expensive maintenance contracts, so many bundle customer support into the basic offer subscription price. Customers who twist these XaaS suppliers' arms to get services such as implementation or training thrown into the contract at the last minute are often successful. The XaaS executives are confident the profits will be there mañana. For right now, they prioritize the booking.

In Chapter 2, we asserted that Marc Benioff and Jeff Bezos probably believe that they could be highly profitable now if they needed to. We are almost certain they believe in mañana profits. But what we hear from the traditional high-tech companies that zero in on salesforce.com as the poster child of unprofitability is that Mr. Benioff claimed strong profits were right around the corner—and has been making that same claim for years. But it hasn't happened. It's not just Benioff and Bezos; it's nearly everyone in this business model. Sure Oracle paid billions for Taleo, and SAP did the same for SuccessFactors. Both acquisitions were high growth, but neither was profitable. Look at the analysis shown in Figure 3.7, which compares growth and operating margins for many of the big names in both traditional and XaaS B2B business models over the three years from 2009 through 2012.

In this figure,[5] the size of the circle indicates the size of the company. You can see the big IBM circle and the much smaller Rackspace one, for example. As a collective group of companies, the average three-year CAGR (compound annual growth rate) was 12.3%, and the average operating margin was 16.9% (these averages are represented by the perpendicular lines in the middle of the chart). But just as in our TSIA indexes, two things jump out at you. The first is that all the companies that were growing faster than the average (the lower-right quadrant) are XaaS models except Nuance. The second is that all the companies that were more profitable than the average (the upper-left quadrant) were traditional, on-prem suppliers during this period.

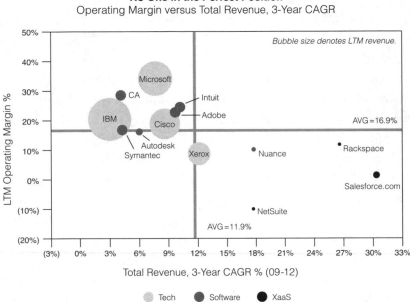

No One in the Perfect Position
Operating Margin versus Total Revenue, 3-Year CAGR

FIGURE 3.7 No Perfect Position: Operating Margin versus Total Revenue, 3-Year CAGR

But the big, startling, frustrating revelation for suppliers in both camps is this: No one was above average in both (the upper-right quadrant). Of the companies we looked at, there is not a single B2B tech supplier that was both high growth and high profit. Not one.

So if you were the CEO of Microsoft, could you really go to Wall Street and tell people that you are moving to the lower right? That you were prepared to trade off profits for growth? That would be a tough investor briefing. Even just making a simple pricing change from up-front license to ongoing subscription has proved to be a tough road. Symantec, Adobe, Autodesk, and Intuit have all begun the move—four traditional B2B software companies courageous enough to begin their move off the Status Quo quadrant in our 2 × 2 matrix toward the XaaS one. All four have experienced bumps on the road to satisfying investors because of the lower up-front revenue of the subscription model and/or lower profitability compared with their previous "status quo" levels.

So it begs two fundamental questions: The first one is whether the business and operating model currently known as XaaS is really the new model that suppliers seek. The second is whether the current iteration of the model really makes much difference for customers beyond how they pay and who owns the asset. We think the answer to both questions in the long run is no. We think current XaaS models are waypoints, not a destination. We think there is another new model emerging (see Figure 3.8).

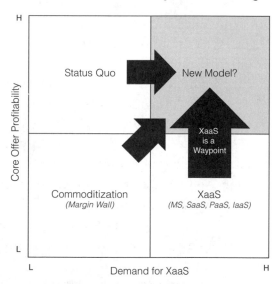

We Believe There Is a Truly New Model in Sight

FIGURE 3.8 A Truly New Model in Sight

So far many suppliers and customers have been "casting about" in their search for that new model. We would submit that the casting about has come from the powerful gravitational pull of the past. Rather than approaching the problem from the perspective of what's now possible, most large suppliers and customers start by thinking about what minor adjustments can be made to what exists today—their current people, their current investments, and their current processes. In other words, what is the minimum number of changes they must make to the status quo? Even in the case of new companies, the people in leadership often design their practices based on what they have done at previous companies during their career. They may innovatively adapt one or two parts, but the rest looks a lot like standard B2B operating procedures. That is completely understandable. But many of those operating principles are still targeted at an old way of working.

It's the Outcome!

To make a long story short, the search for a "new model" in many high-tech and near-tech industries has been a victim of the Goldilocks principle. Outsourcing was "too heavy," and current XaaS is "too light." We need to find a model that is "just right"— and now we think that time has come. We think the complexity arms race that many high-tech companies have engaged in is dead. Business customers are fed up with paying millions to deploy and maintain the complexity that has been handed to them by suppliers. You probably agree: It's not about hardware and software, or speeds and feeds, or even the number of features anymore.

So the question we will attempt to answer—at least the discussion we want to start—is this: What are we headed *to*? In other words, what is the next generation of technology-fueled, data-driven operating models between business suppliers and their customers?

Before we begin, we want to jump to the end. Once again, history comes to our aid. In 1992, political strategist James Carville was trying to keep all the internal staff members of Bill Clinton's US presidential campaign focused on the keys to winning the election. According to legend, he hung a sign in Clinton's campaign headquarters that read: "It's the economy, stupid." Maybe tech suppliers need to hang up their own internal sign now. Because what matters isn't whether the customer hosts the product or how the pricing works; what matters is the total return they get from those investments—the outcomes they deliver. *That* is what separates successful CIOs from unsuccessful ones, profitable hospitals from unprofitable ones, and high-efficiency manufacturers from low-efficiency ones. In a rapidly maturing tech industry, it's about the outcome! And both sides of the B2B divide are about to have a chance to partner much more effectively to unlock its full potential.

Here is our pass at what the evolution of B2B might look like.

4 | B4B

EVEN IN THE NEXT GENERATION OF B2B THERE WILL STILL BE A divide to bridge between the daily self-interest of a supplier and that of its business customers. What we would like to propose is a more modern way to think about how that bridge should be constructed.

In our framework, which we call "B4B" to contrast it with Patterson's original B2B, it does not matter what the product is or what it does. It could be simple or complex, cheap or expensive, hardware or software, this industry or that . . . it doesn't matter. Similarly, our model is indifferent to the outcome the customer wishes to achieve. Once again, it is whatever it is. That means you can choose pretty much any example you want. If you are a supplier, you can use your own products and target any market. If you are a business customer, you can choose any current outcome you are trying to achieve and consider any supplier's product that might help you get there.

B4B is based on the idea that a supplier's operating model will soon play a far greater role in bridging the chasm between the product's capabilities and the customer's desired outcome. There is great, unleashed power trapped within most suppliers. Until recently, it really wasn't feasible to bring that power to market at scale, nor was it in demand. But a great product combined with a powerful supplier operating model is going to trump a great product alone every time. In the old world, suppliers sold things *to* customers—that's what the 2 in B2B stands for. In the new world, suppliers are also going to start doing things *for* customers—that's what the 4 in B4B stands for. Customers are going to demand more involvement from their suppliers to ensure that the value they were promised is fully delivered.

Basic B4B Construct

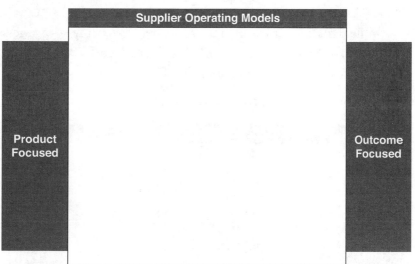

FIGURE 4.1 Basic B4B Construct

As shown in Figure 4.1, the supplier's operating model will either add value or not add value to what the product could achieve on its own. In theory, a business customer could find a product lying in the street with the manufacturer's name scratched out and probably still get some value out of it. But customers don't usually operate that way. They don't usually buy technology at auctions or from newspaper ads. They buy technology from suppliers whom they expect to play some kind of role in the outcome that product delivers. It is this role that we're talking about. Is it a little or a lot? Is it useful or not? Although that may sound simplistic to you, we believe it is anything but. We think billions will be spent on suppliers trying to differentiate on this point. We also argue that it is where some of the most profound innovations of the cloud will occur. As we have highlighted, there are many interesting, potentially disruptive, models floating around in the B2C world—and on the edges of the B2B world. Taken as a group, they represent pioneering efforts to transform the old model. But importantly, what we see at TSIA when we look across all of these efforts is a series of patterns.

Power Lines

We think that the future operating model that bridges business customers to their suppliers will be characterized by two simple elements that we call Power Lines (see Figure 4.2).

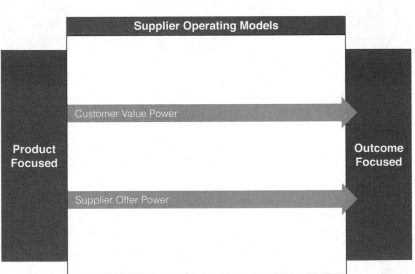

FIGURE 4.2 The Two Power Lines of B4B

Power Lines don't refer just to the inherent potential of the product itself, but also to the combined power of the product plus the operating model between the supplier and the customer. The two Power Lines of B4B each take a different perspective.

The first one focuses on how much opportunity exists to add to the product's value:

- **Customer Value Power:** Customers articulate business value in many ways, but at the end of the day, every description resolves down to just three dimensions: increasing my revenues, lowering my costs, and reducing my risk. Some successful solutions have an impact on all three, some on just two, and a few have an impact on only one of these dimensions of business value. The key question considered by Customer Value Power: *Is there an opportunity for the supplier's operating model to have a positive impact on the three dimensions of customer value?*

The second Power Line focuses on whether a supplier can credibly provide the right kind of help:

- **Supplier Offer Power:** Just because there is the opportunity for the supplier to help the customer improve these significant outcomes does not mean the supplier has an offer aimed at doing it. The key question considered by Supplier Offer Power: *How much outcome power has this supplier added to their standard product via complementary offers—what you might call "value amplification"?*

We think these two simple Power Lines can be used to structure a meaningful conversation not only about how suppliers and customers partner today, but also about how they will partner in the future. To accomplish this, we also need to frame in a finite number of points on each Power Line.

Supplier Levels

The B4B construct calls out four levels of suppliers, as shown in Figure 4.3. At each level, we seek to find the proper balance between the opportunities to assist customers on the top Power Line with the available offers of suppliers on the bottom one.

The Four Supplier Levels of B4B

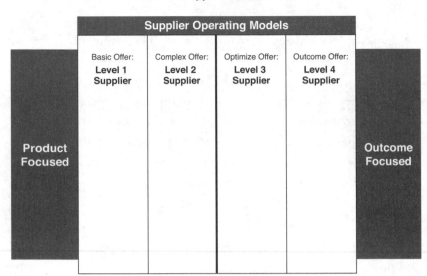

FIGURE 4.3 The Four Supplier Levels of B4B

We will explain the four supplier levels as we go, so without further ado, let's get to work using the model. We start our discussion at Level 1 because that is where the traditional B2B model can be found.

The Level 1 Supplier

B2B suppliers historically wanted to stay close to their products. We think Level 1 was what Patterson envisioned. His standard-setting operating model for NCR was really not based on adding much value beyond the product's capabilities (see Figure 4.4). It was designed to get the maximum number of products into the market and then, based on their inherent feature set, let those products do their job. This is still the approach that many B2B suppliers employ. It features highly scalable, low-friction attributes. Just make, sell, and ship. Many suppliers like the thought that if you control your sales force and your manufacturing quality, you can roll from deal to deal without being bogged down in the specific needs or demands of individual customers.

The Four Supplier Levels of B4B
Level 1: Basic Offer Supplier

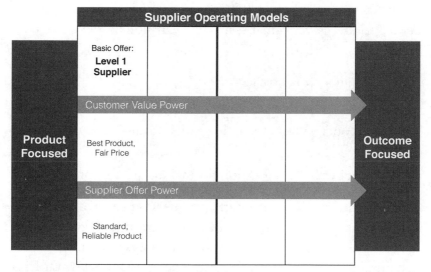

FIGURE 4.4 Level 1: Basic Offer Supplier

Importantly, Level 1 is *exactly* the right supplier level for many kinds of B2B purchases. Business customers procure products and services every day that are either very simple to own and operate or are very well understood by their internal staff. In these cases, customers do not really require much support from the operating model of the supplier, and they certainly wouldn't want to pay extra for it. It might be because there is not much variability risk in the outcome, or because the outcome itself is not that critical.

Think of Level 1 as being appropriate for basic offers. There are many examples that should come to mind when you think about Level 1 offers. They include all the simple products a business needs: office supplies, furniture, and delivery trucks. They might also include products whose operation is very simple, regardless of price, and products that, once turned on, just run and run with little or no intervention. Think about mechanical things such as valves or tools, even some basic electronics such as two-way radios. You could even include slightly more advanced products—ones that a business customer uses regularly and employees can easily operate—maybe a forklift or an X-ray machine.

In these cases, the need for supplier involvement via its operating model is very small—maybe even nonexistent. The customer only asks that:

- the product works well.
- the purchase price is a fair one.
- the product continues to be widely available as a standard offer.
- the supplier has a reputation for making reliable products.

These are the classic demands of customers on basic offers. However, these are also offers that can rapidly commoditize. The unit gross margins can become quite low. Suppliers may only survive and prosper at Level 1 if they have an operating model that is frictionless and scalable. They need to sell high volumes of standardized products and be confident that they will operate satisfactorily with minimal involvement after the sale. It is a manufacturer's view of how B2B should work. They want the customer's focus on the product, not on the services or the company.

Right here—right at this point—is when trouble can and has begun. You see, the definition of which products are truly well suited to this "frictionless" supplier level is being stretched. It is suppliers who are doing that stretching. Level 1 works when the products are simple for the customer to master and when the outcome is almost a sure thing. But as software eats the world, fewer and fewer products are that simple. Complexity and the consumption gap have blossomed in the world of B2B. They are not the friends of a frictionless, scalable operating model for suppliers. Yet most product companies yearn for that model. It is here, at the intersection of growing technical complexity and a legacy desire for suppliers to remain frictionless, that the old B2B model perishes. It is not what Patterson built it for. For many product categories, Level 1 is simply running out of gas. But more on this subject in a minute.

The Level 2 Supplier

We don't think Level 2 was designed by anyone. It just grew.

We just reviewed the fundamental premises of Level 1. We believe that Level 2 grew out of Level 1—one painful lesson at a time (see Figure 4.5). At some point in the life of suppliers, they have a problem with a big customer. Maybe the product they purchased was too hard to set up, or it didn't work right, or it was failing too often. So the customer goes back to the supplier and says, "Hey! This isn't OK. Fix it," and the supplier does. If it only happens once in a great while, the supplier fixes it as an exception. If it happens a lot, the supplier gets into the service business.

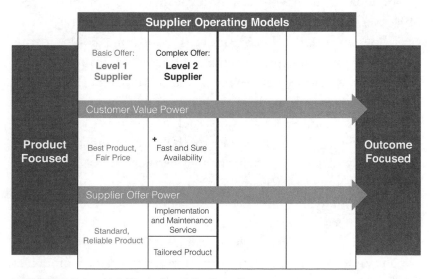

FIGURE 4.5 Level 2: Complex Offer Supplier

A Level 2 supplier is a company—a software provider, a manufacturer, or a reseller—that knows there will always be a huge gap between shipping a product to a customer and having that customer successfully operate that product. There is a gap of time, a gap of resources, and a gap of expertise. At this point, complexity introduces new value elements into the traditional B2B equation. It is no longer just a basic offer. The product's inherent value still exists, and ultimately the customer could get to benefit from that value. It still needs to be reliable, fairly priced, and so on—all the attributes of Level 1. That is what the + sign in the model indicates. But now the proliferation of features, capabilities, and complexity means that the customer needs a lot of help to get to that value and stay there. Each day that they can't and don't is value lost. Thus, the Customer Value Power Line is extended for Level 2 suppliers. It is not just about the product anymore; it is about how fast and how efficiently the customer can realize value by getting—and keeping—the product available and operational.

In addition to having unique expertise to accomplish these objectives, Level 2 suppliers also offer customers an attractive labor-sourcing model. Theoretically, the customer could go out and hire an army of experts on that product to get it into production. But it would be very expensive and inefficient. They don't want a permanent labor base with those skills; just a temporary one. A Level 2 supplier acts as just such a source.

So at Level 2, suppliers add to their operating model. Either directly or through their channel partners, Level 2 suppliers offer professional services, education services, and support services. They may also offer services to tailor the product to the customer's needs. In short, they must now evidence that they have added service credibility to their brand.

Taken together, the customer-supplier operating model at Level 2 looks far different from that at Level 1. Customers have new things to consider, suppliers have new capabilities in which they must invest. Almost every traditional enterprise software company uses a Level 2 supplier model.

Trouble in Paradise

As we just mentioned, companies on both sides of the great divide run into trouble if a supplier brings a complex offer (Level 2) to the market but tries to stick to a basic supplier (Level 1) operating model.

You have experienced this multiple times in your personal life. You buy a wireless printer for your home and then spend all weekend trying to get the darned thing to work. That's because the printer's manufacturer is operating at very low prices and margins. It is clinging to the frictionless, scalable Level 1 model. But the fact is that the product is not that easy to master. It is not basic. It is complex. You find yourself alone, frustrated, and ready to take it back. The manufacturer refused to accept that if it wanted to play in the complex offer category, it needed to move to a Level 2 operating model. Someone *should* have been there to help you. Someone *should* have filled the time and expertise gaps around the product. But no one did. Or maybe the Level 1 supplier was so addicted to the frictionless model that its management buried its head in the sand and just prayed its reseller channel would provide the Level 2 services around the product. In doing so, it lost control of service quality.

That exact same thing happens when software eats the world of a near-tech industry. Products that used to be installed using a wrench are now configured with software. Forklifts driven by people are being replaced with robots that must be "taught" the warehouse floor plan and traffic patterns. Valves that shut down water pipes must now be connected to the Internet. Delivery trucks are repaired with laptops. These are but a few examples of Level 1 suppliers that are being dragged, often kicking and screaming, into Level 2. Many resist. They like being frictionless. They want to remain manufacturers, not become service providers. They don't want to replace the instruction manual with a temperamental field software engineer. But they must move to Level 2; otherwise, their customers will fail.

As we said, the root problem was that the "supply push" operating model of early Level 1 manufacturers was not sufficiently updated for life at Level 2. These were companies that correctly believed that features sold products. The sales and R&D heads atop their B2B totem poles dominated their strategy brain. They prioritized features over serviceability. That worked fine for simpler, more mechanical, more self-contained products. But that is not what Level 2 suppliers are making today. Yet at many of these companies, that mentality still prevails. It is ironic that one key part of the world that software has not done a great job of eating so far is around automating the configuration, deployment, and maintenance of complex technology. It might not be much of a stretch to say that suppliers spend $10 engineering new features into today's complex offers for every $1 they spend engineering out the huge service requirements that accompany them.

The result has been a rapid increase in customer spending on complexity services. As we said before, we don't think anyone actually designed the Level 2 supplier operating model—it just grew. The problem is that it never stopped. We have already pointed out the huge amount of spending, particularly in high-tech, on product-attached services. Hundreds of billions of dollars are being spent by business customers to get complex offers operational and to keep them that way. We are hearing about software deployments in which customers are spending 5 to 10 times as much on deployment services as they did for the software itself. As more and more near-tech industries become software driven, their customers can expect the same thing. You see, so far, service spending has chased complexity. And complexity knows no boundaries.

In Chapter 1, we noted that many business customers have willingly accepted this somewhat unusual partnership arrangement. It seems strange that suppliers can hand off incredibly complex offers to customers and then charge them vast amounts of money to deal with it. No one did it intentionally. Like proverbial frogs that start in a pot full of cold water and slowly have the heat turned up on them, both sides were victims of the complexity arms race. There was definitely value in these services; it has just gotten out of control. Services are a great way to spend money and they are going to be a central figure in Levels 3 and 4. However, we think they will be different kinds of services. Apple acts as a phenomenal example of a supplier that has engineered out many sources of product complexity, thus reducing the need for lots of traditional tech support. Instead, it offers new kinds of services that really increase the value of its products to customers.

In summary, Level 2 has Level 1 as its mother and complexity as its father. Together they parented the supplier operating model adopted by tens of thousands of high-tech and near-tech product providers today. Like all children, it has its strengths and its weaknesses. More thought probably could and should have gone into it early on, especially as it chased complexity to the stars. Now, we are about to cross over into the next era. There is still complexity living at this new level, so we think it's a transformation whose design calls for active participation—"imagineering," as Walt Disney would have called it—from both sides of the great divide.

The Level 3 Supplier

If you look carefully at Figure 4.6, you will see a very hard line in B4B between Levels 2 and 3. That's because it represents a real breakthrough in the evolution of B2B. We think it is the new model that many supplier CEOs seek but sometimes struggle to articulate simply.

You might even say that the separation between Levels 2 and 3 is not made up of one hard line but two. The first is that being a Level 3 supplier means that you are willing not only to retain all the same focus on your product that you would at Level 1 or Level 2, but that you are also willing to cross over the dangerous line into playing an active role in optimizing the customer's actual outcome. Believe us, this is a decision that makes many suppliers gulp hard. Historically, suppliers could largely control the cost of

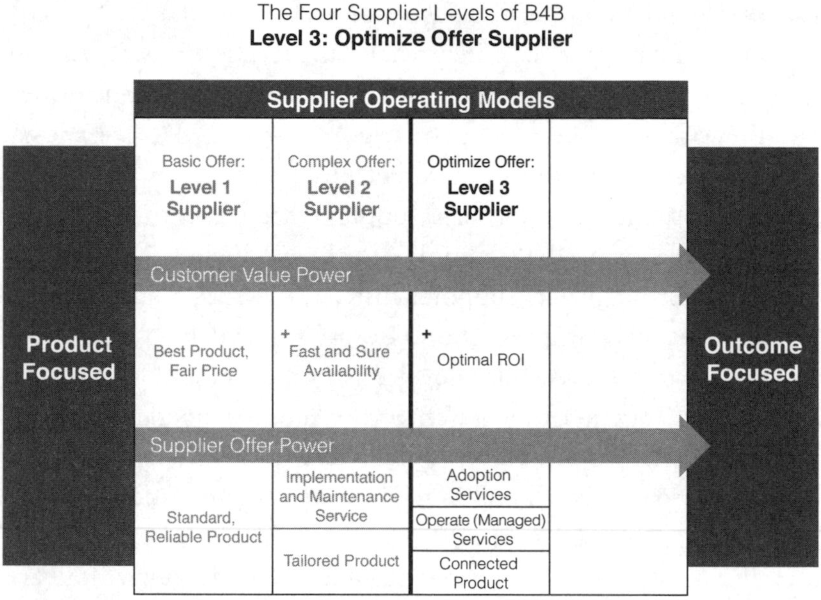

The Four Supplier Levels of B4B
Level 3: Optimize Offer Supplier

Supplier Operating Models			
Basic Offer: **Level 1 Supplier**	Complex Offer: **Level 2 Supplier**	Optimize Offer: **Level 3 Supplier**	

Customer Value Power →

Product Focused

| Best Product,
Fair Price | +
Fast and Sure
Availability | +
Optimal ROI | |

Outcome Focused

Supplier Offer Power →

Standard, Reliable Product	Implementation and Maintenance Service	Adoption Services	
		Operate (Managed) Services	
	Tailored Product	Connected Product	

FIGURE 4.6 Level 3: Optimize Offer Supplier

their products and the services surrounding them. Crossing that line into involvement with the customer outcome meant you had to dive deep into each customer's unique situation. In short, the supplier had to absorb some of the customer's complexity. Crossing that line also meant deploying people, usually expensive ones, to optimize the outcome in question. A double gulp, if you will. These types of customer-supplier arrangements just weren't scalable; they were full of friction and labor.

But today we are sitting on the brink of the new era of B4B—an era that will be defined by suppliers who knowingly and enthusiastically jump in side by side with customers in order to optimize the outcomes they can achieve with the supplier's product. The technology, the world's digital wiring, and the data and analytics—they are all there now. For the first time, all the ingredients are on the table to make something remarkable happen.

How will it be different? Let's use the Power Lines to frame it.

At Level 3, the Customer Value Power Line is extended again. At this level, the supplier's operating model begins to pursue a new objective: helping customers extract the maximum ROI from the product. As we know, there are many dimensions to the pursuit of this worthy goal. Customer outcomes can be influenced, positively or negatively, by everything from system performance optimization to usage levels to data quality. Imagine a supplier that starts not only monitoring the performance of its own products, but also the key performance indicators (KPIs) of the customer teams with which it works. Or maybe the supplier starts monitoring the customer's surrounding quality, efficiency, or customer satisfaction KPIs and has the tools and charter to improve them. The opportunity to optimize the customer's outcome in these ways is enormous. With a little help from their suppliers, customers may be able to increase the total ROI from a technology investment by 20% or 50% or more!

The supplier's operating model can also extend into the customer's total cost of ownership. As everyone knows, the amount a business customer pays for a product and its maintenance fees is only part of its total cost of ownership (TCO). In high-tech companies, there are armies of IT specialists needed to keep internal systems operating at peak productivity. In near-tech companies, there are similar job roles for systems engineers or operators who are specially trained to keep manufacturing lines running or medical equipment safe and productive. There may also be efficiency or quality experts employed by the customer who are tasked with extracting just a little more value out of the asset or the system of which it is a component. These TCOs easily run into the millions or tens of millions of dollars for even mid-sized business customers. The ability of suppliers to take on an active, daily role in reducing these costs is a unique and powerful opportunity to contribute to the customer's overall outcome.

However, like the move to Level 2, Level 3 suppliers must now evidence new capabilities. Their Supplier Offer Power must clearly indicate their enthusiasm and readiness to play new roles in the partnership. As we'll discuss at length in the next chapter, suppliers must have a strategy for connecting to their technology product. On top of this connection, they can build new service offers such as remote operate or managed services that help optimize the customer's technical operation of the product. They might soon include new adoption services to plan, monitor, and optimize the end business users' adoption of its key features. In the past, such tasks would only have been achieved by the customers themselves or by having some of the supplier's employees on the customer's site, as they did in the world of outsourcing or in early versions of managed services. But today those things are possible using data and analytics, sensors, and cloud-based intervention techniques. It is a big change, but it is happening in more instances by more suppliers in more industries every day. It takes time to build the capabilities and to perfect their delivery. If they are the OEM, suppliers must also work out what roles their channel partners will play and what they will do directly. But if business customers don't see those offers somewhere in the supplier's ecosystem, they should question the promises made by its salespeople. Although Level 3 suppliers are not in a position to guarantee the outcome, they are certainly going to deliver far better results to customers than what they could achieve on their own. There are great examples of Level 3 offers out there today such as GE Healthcare's Hospital Operations Management System and Avaya's Unified Communications Managed Services.

These new roles can feel a bit unnatural, even for SaaS and other XaaS providers. Maybe that uneasiness is because they are a XaaS start-up led by executives who come from Level 2 backgrounds and who were conditioned to avoid these services due to their friction and labor costs. Or maybe they are a traditional, on-prem Level 2 supplier building out their first XaaS offers. In either case, it may be tempting for them to believe that their twin, end-goal innovations are cloud hosting their "multi-tenant" product and then offering it with subscription pricing. We don't think so. As we mentioned, those are critical aspects of Level 3—important but insufficient. Wrap an XaaS product in the traditional services of a Level 2 supplier, and all you have done is change who hosts it. Take a Level 2 product and wrap it in a subscription pricing model, and your deep-pocketed competitors can copy it in a month. Make the full move to being a Level 3 supplier, and you may double or triple the Customer Value Power of your offer.

But Level 3 is not without its controversies. We submit that to be an effective Level 3 supplier, one that can truly operate in this model, you need to be able to evidence the capability to secure the customer access you are asking for. As we just pointed out, in order to help optimize customers' ROI or reduce their TCO, you will need to be connected: connected to devices, connected to data, and connected to employees. That's a big request of business customers—one that can rightly make them very nervous. They may fear leaks of proprietary information or whether sharing such data complies with legal requirements. But here is the bottom line: If business customers and their suppliers cannot work this out, then the tremendous benefits available to both parties by operating at Level 3 will be out of reach. They will simply be impractical to achieve, at least not at any scale. If business customers won't allow this model into their facilities, they are destined to go it alone. It is a trade-off, a hard one. Although both sides must attack the problem by working together, the onus is on suppliers to take the lead. How can they protect the customers' information better than customers can themselves? What rules can they offer up for engaging directly with end users? What limits and notifications can they offer for the direct operation or optimization of equipment? What walls will be built so that customers' own data are not "used against them" in the pricing of the next deal? These are the tough questions that suppliers must answer. They are the new additions to a Level 3 supplier's brand criteria.

Level 3 will draw on breakthroughs from across the worlds of B2B and B2C. It is in its infancy today. However, you can expect a rapid pace of evolution. Now is the time for us to have the debate. Now is the time for suppliers and customers to work out exactly how their Level 3 relationship is going to work. As we have said, complexity still lives at Level 3, so don't just let it grow. Envision it, plan it, and work it. For the first time, both parties can stand side by side on a daily basis to optimize the business results from a technology investment. It is immensely powerful.

The Level 4 Supplier

Level 4 represents the theoretical end game for suppliers. They now offer a true, no-risk/no-use/no-pay offer. It's a glamorous option for customers: They don't buy assets or manage complexity. At Level 4, they are purely buying an outcome. For suppliers, it can be either financially glamorous or too dangerous to handle. If the supplier has truly automated a domain—the B2B equivalent of a B2C experience—it can be great. But if it is just a gutsy willingness to absorb Level 2 complexity and risk as a pricing maneuver, it can be very tricky.

To succeed profitably, Level 4 suppliers must request that the customer does things their way—even if that means changing the way that customer operated in the past. In return, the supplier promises to ease and de-risk the domain, charging only for consumption or even the sharing of gains, not demanding huge upfront commitments. They seem to be saying, "Don't think about things in the old way, think about them in a new way. If you will let us, we can change the game for you financially or competitively." But a Level 4 supplier must be totally confident they have truly mastered their domain and its complexity.

Historically, the players who may come to mind as typically making "outcome offers" might be the outsourcing companies. You might even broaden the list to include system integrators or even a few consulting firms. These "pure service" companies featured a team of smart people who could take over a process, add some labor and technology, and then operate it for the customer. Or maybe they would build it, operate it, and then transfer it back to the customer once it was fully optimized and the outcome was assured. In that respect, they serve as easy-to-understand symbols of the kinds of opportunities and capabilities that exist at this level. However, at least in their traditional "custom project" forms, they are not what we mean by Level 4 suppliers. Now don't get us wrong, many of these pure service firms are indeed headed this way by investing in all the empowering capabilities we are about to discuss. But what might surprise them when they arrive at what we classify as Level 4 is that there are tons of new players in the "outcome" market. Many of these newcomers may not have believed just a few years before that they wanted to play at this level. They could not imagine a model with more friction, higher labor costs, and less scalability. These reluctant new entrants are product companies. Let us tell you a short story that explains why the market may soon encourage them to re-think that position.

A few years ago, one of the authors gave a presentation to the senior executives at a $9 billion tech company. Just before he stood up, the head of R&D had been proudly talking about the nearly 600 new features in the latest release of a key software application. While both were standing, the author provoked a discussion about why 600 new features were needed. Well, it turns out that most of them had been added in order to win specific deals. It seems that this new customer wanted these eight things added, and that this new customer wanted these 16 things changed, and so forth. Add all of those customization requests together, and you could account for the vast majority of the 600. At that point, the author pushed a bit further. "How many customers around the world use your systems today to perform its particular business function?" he asked. The answer was in the thousands. "How many years have you been in this business?" he asked next. It was dozens. "How many world-class experts in your particular solution area do you employ?" he continued. It was hundreds. Finally he asked, "Who knows more about how to optimize a business customer's outcomes in your particular domain area, you or one of those customers who was demanding lots of customization?" There were heads shaking around the table.

The answer was clearly that the supplier knew more about the particular business domain that is the subject of their products and services. Yet on a deal-by-deal basis, their salespeople were often succumbing to the way the potential customer did business in the past. They often failed to win the customer over to the idea that they could actually coach their business processes, even their business model, to a new level of performance. We didn't know what to call it then, but now we would say that they had many of the basic ingredients to act as a Level 4 supplier.

Simply put, a Level 4 supplier is one that is confident they can deliver a specific outcome for a business customer "as a service" (see Figure 4.7). As we said, it is another brave move for product suppliers—especially since they may take deals where pricing is tied directly to the outcome. It is also a brave move for the customers who put their trust in them. But when a supplier can truly do that, their Power Lines extend. The Customer Value outcomes become easier for the customer to attain. Level 4 offers may be game-changing, bringing important new capabilities, eliminating wide bands of fixed cost, or changing the way the customer operates to ensure better results in a specific area.

Product companies, if they can truly leverage their concentrated domain focus, may have a competitive advantage over pure service companies at Level 4. They have a head start brought about by their very broad base of very focused experiences. Product suppliers can draw from an "n of many" rather than an "n of few." In a traditional consulting or outsourcing engagement, customers usually benefit from one or two senior partners and/ or executives who have done similar engagements before and use that experience to guide the teams doing the actual work on the

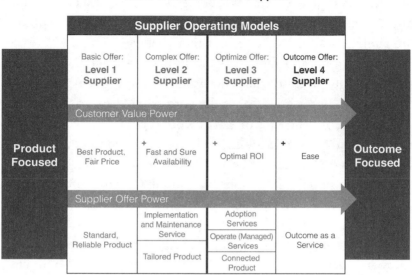

The Four Supplier Levels of B4B
Level 4: Outcome Offer Supplier

FIGURE 4.7 Level 4: Outcome Offer Supplier

project. But when product companies truly harness the power of their domain expertise, they can bring a far broader base of best practice experience, such as facts about what really works and what really doesn't.

Second, they orient toward technology and products, not toward labor. Game-changing results are hard to separate from game-changing technology these days. One of the things that can distinguish a true Level 4 supplier from a traditional pure service company is that they are not trying to spin up a mile of custom code or put as many bodies on the customer's site as possible. A profitable Level 4 supplier evidences their Supplier Offer Power primarily through a standard technology platform, not labor.

Although Level 4 is the newest and most fluid of all supplier levels, we think customers can expect to see two main variations of offers. One is the most glamorous of supplier strategies, the other the most dangerous. They both represent a claim by a supplier that they can master their domain. The most glamorous Level 4 claim being made in B2B high-tech today is full automation. Rackspace and AWS are popular brands seeking to be the new face of fully automated Level 4 offers. It is also where many new SaaS entrants are aiming—though they are not there yet.

The second and most dangerous Level 4 offer is the "all-in bundle." This promises the same value proposition of "outcome as a service," but it is far from fully automated. Instead it is a bundle of traditional Level 2 or Level 3 product and service components offered as a single package with pricing tied to consumption or outcomes. Despite still being complex, the Level 4 supplier is willing to assume that complexity and take almost all of the risk. We will cover Level 4 platform offers in a bit more detail in the next chapter.

So we believe that you will, at least you should, see more and more suppliers starting to play at Level 4. Level 4 is not about custom projects. It is about reusable outcome platforms in targeted domains. Here, product companies have an advantage.

A couple notes of caution based on the lessons of the past may be in order. The first caution is for customers. Just like the problems caused by Level 1 suppliers that offered a product that required Level 2 services but weren't willing to fund them, you must carefully evaluate your Level 4 supplier candidates. Offering outcome-as-a-service reliably, profitably, and at scale requires suppliers to truly commit. They must have the processes, agreements, people, data, analytics, tools, and software to transform the vast experience of customers, partners, and employees into a tight body of knowledge or a platform of technology—some form of codified domain expertise. It's one thing to have a few great individual service people who can get good customer outcomes, but it's another to have "industrialized" it. When any supplier, whether offering a product or a pure service, says it plays at this level, customers should be able to feel that industrialization. If not, customers should be prepared to get out their wallet and their patience. Checking the supplier's customer references is critical.

There is risk to both sides when a supplier says it plays at Level 4 when it really doesn't. A true Level 4 supplier has mastered its domain and it has mastered its complexity. Short of that, Level 4 is not the right place to play.

Supplier caution is also called for. You must carefully evaluate the risks at this level. First, if customers do not achieve their outcome and the deal pricing is based solely on consumption or gain sharing, the supplier has all the risk. The only way to avoid a loss in that case is if the platform has almost no incremental cost to serve that customer. That is why full automation offers can be far more aggressive in taking on new customers in this model compared to all-in bundles. Second, as the lesson of office product companies taught us in Chapter 3, simple per-unit pricing can commoditize rapidly. If the Level 4 supplier goes for true "as-a-service pricing," meaning that it no longer charges separately for customer support, managed services, or other component offers, it runs the risk of the service becoming unprofitable as price wars drive down unit prices. If that happens, the supplier has no other revenue streams to fall back on.

And, Not Or

So these are the four supplier levels of B4B. Put simply, we are on the brink of a new generation of technology-fueled, data-driven operating models that have the potential to radically improve the returns that business customers receive from their technology investments. Taken together, we think the B4B framework is a simple, useful way to structure the transformation conversations that need to take place inside suppliers and with their customers.

While they may not have used our B4B terminology until now, many B2B product suppliers today may be finding their collective strategy brain tied up in knots trying to figure out at which supplier level they need to play. Should a high-tech supplier that is profitable but growing slowly stay at Level 2 or move to Level 3? If a near-tech company starts to add more software to its product, should it jump seriously into Level 2, or can it cling a bit longer to Level 1? Is a Level 3 company ready to make the brave move to Level 4's all-in, no-risk-to-the-customer pricing models?

To those suppliers we say one important thing: This is not a matter of one level *or* another. This is a matter of one level *and* another. There will be certain products in certain customer markets for which being a Level 1 supplier is perfect because the customer can take the product and run with it. But for a growing number of suppliers, there are going to be other products or other customer markets for which Level 3 is the big opportunity. There will even be cases in which the exact same product enters different markets and uses different operating models to meet the needs of those specific types of customers, offering them a stairway to value. What is critical is that suppliers recognize when they need to master multiple supplier levels, and then be able to smartly assign the right one to each product market opportunity. We think it will be very rare for a company to play at a single supplier level. It is not this one *or* that one for most suppliers. It is this one *and* that one.

Successful B4B suppliers will have mastered the Goldilocks problem. They will be able to crisply identify the required operating model for each market. They won't sloppily back their way into one supplier level from the previous one; they will run forward with great excitement and confidence because they understand their role, their offer, and how it adds value. In short, they will do each one "just right."

The Great Migrations

But even though we just made the point that many suppliers will need to play at multiple levels simultaneously, we have to admit that we don't think all four levels will enjoy equal levels of prosperity in the future. As we'll explain in Chapter 10, we would assert that the tea leaves are becoming easier to read. There are going to be some major migrations affecting huge herds of suppliers as they follow the changing rivers of customer money.

Migration Paths in B4B

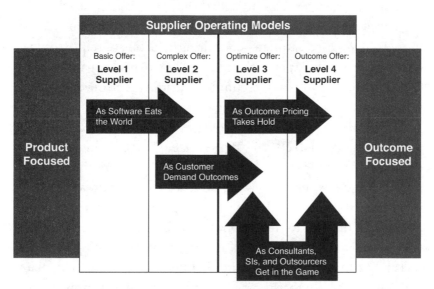

FIGURE 4.8 Migration Paths in the B4B Construct

Based on our engagement with the current operating models at so many companies, we think the next few years will demand a shift to the right for almost every high-tech and near-tech supplier. As shown in Figure 4.8, we believe that many traditional product manufacturers will be dragged from Level 1 to Level 2 as their products increase in both capability and complexity, becoming near-tech suppliers. They will need to create new and substantive service offers as a result. Their revenue mix will shift as these new services grow faster than the products do. At the same time, Level 2 suppliers, particularly high-tech ones, are already starting to be measured differently by some customers who are challenging them to reduce the complexity that has grown out of proportion to business results. Level 2 suppliers will be increasingly held accountable for optimizing outcomes, not just supplying technology. The really smart ones will see the enormous potential to differentiate around that demand. They will find new services that take commoditizing technologies and de-commoditize them. They will flock to the new categories of customer spend in areas such as managed services. In short, they will *run* to Level 3, not be forced into it. As Level 3 becomes the preferred partnership model for many customers, consulting and outsourcing companies will also want a piece of the pie. They may also partner with OEMs or build their own technology platforms at Level 4. Either way, they will want to be in the game.

We think that one of the most profound impacts of software and the cloud on B2B will be to make Levels 1 and 2 largely transitory states for many suppliers. Level 3 is where the next big action will be, where the rivers of customer money will flow. It just makes too much sense not to. Suppliers know far too much about their domain to sit idly on the sidelines while their customers use trial and error to find their way to success. Suppliers have the ability to efficiently operate technology using one-to-many economies of scale that most individual customers simply cannot achieve. As suppliers expand their base of knowledge by actively engaging in the operations of their customers, they will be in unparalleled positions to create highly valuable Level 4 platforms, but that will take many years in some domains. Level 3 is going to be the big thing for the next several years. It is the threshold level, the beginning of outcome-driven operating models for suppliers—ones that both sides of the great divide can rally around. It is a simple idea that could radically alter the landscape of suppliers and the profitability of their business customers. But although the idea is simple, its execution won't be. We think there are so many opportunities to innovate at this level that both suppliers and customers should redeploy their best and brightest minds to its development.

5 | Connectedness and the Tower of Power

ALTHOUGH THERE WILL CERTAINLY BE VARIATIONS ON THE OPERATING models of successful B4B suppliers, we also think there will be some constant ingredients for success. Two of these ingredients could not be farther apart on the difficulty scale. One is both simple to understand and, in its most basic form, relatively easy to technically execute. The other is really complicated, a multidimensional requirement that is a "tall order" to execute. However, if either one is missing, we would say that the odds are high that the supplier will fail, particularly at Level 3.

These two ingredients are connected products and something we call the Tower of Power. Let's start with the simpler one.

Connectedness

At Level 2, few suppliers know what customers are actually doing with their products. The products themselves are usually physically on the customer's site. Suppliers see them only when service, upgrades, or calibration is required. They may "see" their products by dispatching a field engineer or by having the customer detach the product from its on-premise environment and send it back to the supplier's service facility. If the product is mostly (or all) software, we have learned to "see" the product remotely, which allows suppliers to be proactive in applying bug fixes or minor upgrades.

All of these examples reflect varying, usually primitive, states of connectedness. For some length of time—periodically or constantly—suppliers are once again connected to the product asset that they moved off their balance sheet and onto the customer's. This connection could be powerful, but most of the time it is not. Even most software companies today take powerful Level 3 connection opportunities and do Level 2 things with them, like performing classic technical maintenance functions.

In the future, that connectedness—in every form—will be much more profoundly enabling. As Andreessen pointed out in his 2011 article,[1] the world is becoming digitally wired. In the past, those "wires" used to be limiting. They were physical tethers best suited for stationary devices with easy access to connection points. Today, the existence of low-cost, wireless broadband opens up opportunities to connect more and more things in more and more places. Let's take a look at a couple of extreme examples of connectedness.

In 2001 Japanese electronics maker Zojirushi Corporation began offering a product and service called "i-pot." Basically, it makes tea; it's an electric kettle with a decidedly modern twist. The i-pot (for information pot) not only boils water for instant miso soup and green tea, but it also records the times the user pushes a button and dispenses the water. A wireless communication device at the bottom of the i-pot sends a signal to a server. Members of the service can see recent records of i-pot usage on a website. In addition, twice a day, the server e-mails the three most recent usage times to a designated recipient.

Why is all that functionality useful? Because in the "graying Japan" of 2001, more than one-third of households had members older than 65, and 4.8 million households were composed of elderly couples. An additional 3.4 million people lived alone. In Tokyo in the prior 10 years, the number of deaths among the unattended elderly had doubled.[2] The i-pot offered a simple way to connect elderly family members with their loved ones multiple times each day. The connection was technically simple but powerfully important.

GE is also working on staying connected to its products. But many of their products are not sitting passively in someone's kitchen. One of the things that GE connects to in real time could be moving 500 miles per hour at 39,000 feet over the Pacific Ocean. According to GE there are more than 40,000 jet engines in the commercial airline fleet worldwide and another 10 times that many in the military and noncommercial fleets. In addition to moving fast and traveling high, these engines also have critical components that spin—fast. Each engine has a turbine fan, a compressor, and a turbine. Each must be instrumented separately and constantly monitored. By connecting in real time to these devices, GE can help its aviation customers improve both operations and asset management. It can help them reduce fuel consumption and optimize scheduling. It can anticipate and prevent problems that can extend engine life and limit unscheduled interruptions.[3]

Suppliers that can connect to their products can do amazing things. Yet many suppliers are not doing it today. Even in 2013, we hear a litany of reasons from some tech suppliers about why their products are not connected. Sometimes it's about the limits of their architecture; sometimes it's about the difficult locations or environments their products operate in; and other times, it's about the costs of connecting or the unwillingness of customers to give their permission. But, as shown in Figure 5.1, our logic is this simple.

Cisco calls it the "Internet of Everything." GE calls it the "Industrial Internet." You can call it whatever you want, but the bottom line is this: If you are a B2B supplier and you have an ounce of software in your product, there is really no good excuse not to be connected.

At Level 3, the value of connectedness moves to a whole new level of importance. At Level 2, it enables suppliers to offer preventive and proactive maintenance services. At Level 3, it allows suppliers to increase business customers' revenue, lower their

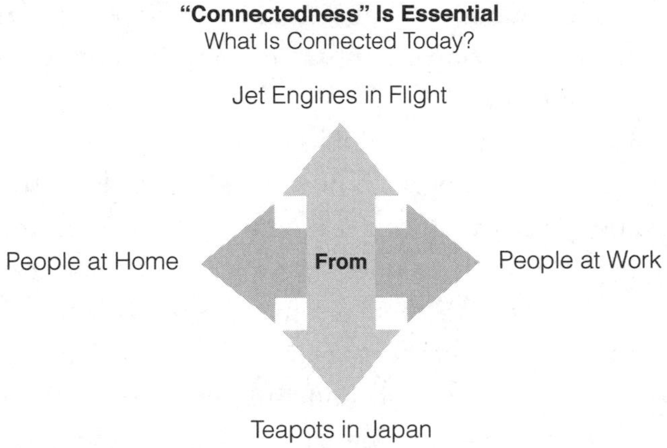

"Connectedness" Is Essential
What Is Connected Today?

Jet Engines in Flight

People at Home   **From**   People at Work

Teapots in Japan

FIGURE 5.1 "Connectedness" Is Essential

labor costs, improve the efficiency of their critical processes, and improve the satisfaction of their end customers. This is not about connectedness as a tactic for reducing suppliers' costs of staying close to their product; this is a profound key to unlocking the true customer value of business technology.

We must admit that we began this chapter with an assertion that was understated. We said that in its most basic form, connectedness should be relatively easy to execute technically. At a basic level, that's probably true. Connecting owners of the i-pot to their loved ones was probably not simple in 2001, but it would be today. Connecting to a device weighing thousands of pounds that has components that spin at 10,000 revolutions per minute while it travels 500 miles per hour over the Pacific? Probably not so simple. We understand that engineering connectivity, particularly the real-time, "always-on," bidirectional kind, may not be simple. And unfortunately it's about to get far more complicated. For, as we'll soon suggest, the design specifications for what that connection must do is about to grow significantly.

The Tower of Power

We could keep the discussion about connectedness short because, if you are a supplier, you already know whether you are connected to the product you have sold to your customer. You know how robust that connection is or why it's not. If you are a business customer, you probably know which of your products are "phoning home" to their supplier and which are not. You also know where you are comfortable with that happening and where you are not. As we have said repeatedly, we think this is something that both sides must work out together or else both will forfeit a great opportunity.

Here is why.

Flowing across this connection—especially at Levels 3 and 4—is going to be a rapidly evolving and important exchange of information we call the Tower of Power. The Tower of Power is not one thing. It is not coming just from the supplier side or just from the customer side. It is admittedly a mixed bag of elements. At the highest level, it is mainly a list of the offers that suppliers need at each level. But those offers are constructed with capabilities, such as product attributes, data access, analytics, frameworks, service resources, and so on. In essence, the Tower of Power is the capability engine of a B4B supplier. Every supplier's version will be unique. The ideas shown in Figure 5.2 are but a few

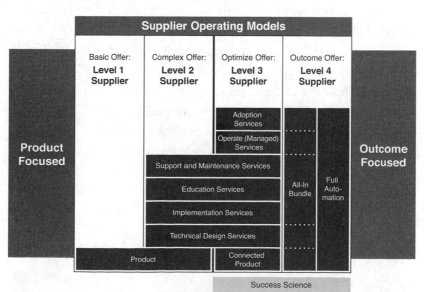

FIGURE 5.2 The Tower of Power

for suppliers to consider building, and for customers to consider connecting to.

The Tower of Power, and the capabilities that fuel it, are what's under the hood of the Supplier Offer Power Line we discussed in Chapter 4. Just as different models of cars need different sizes of engines, so it is with supplier levels. The size and horsepower of each supplier's engine depends on the level or levels at which the supplier intends to play. As we have discussed, Level 1 suppliers rely solely on the inherent value of their product. So they really don't need much of an engine for their operating model. On the other hand, Level 3 suppliers that plan to be actively involved in optimizing their business customers' outcomes need a lot of power under the hood. Thus, our Tower of Power is drawn to show the offers that roughly correspond to the four supplier levels.

Capabilities

To power those offers, we want to introduce the notion of capabilities in the B4B context. At TSIA, we define capabilities as the organizational ability to achieve desired results. They could be processes, skills, metrics, or technologies. So, to continue with our car engine metaphor, under the hood of each offer in the Tower of Power, suppliers will need a specific set of capabilities. As we suggest in the next chapter, this may be the best way for suppliers to manage their progression to new supplier levels.

Before we dig deeper into the tower and some of the required capabilities, let's start by separating the traditional offers of Level 2 suppliers so we can excuse them from further review. In Figure 5.2, if you look at the columns for Level 1 and Level 2 suppliers, you will see product and product-related service offers that should look very familiar:

- Support and maintenance services
- Education services

- Product
- Implementation services
- Technical solutions architecture

If you are a supplier or a business customer, you know them well—how to sell them or how to buy them. As you will see in Figure 5.3, we have grayed out the traditional service offers of Level 2 suppliers, but don't forget: It's *and*, not *or*, so these traditional Level 2 services are still going to be in play at Level 3. They may change, however they won't go away.

But because Level 3 is the future for many of today's Level 2 suppliers, we would like to focus on what we think is going to be new and different for them once they arrive. There are four major things that we think define the Tower of Power at Level 3, as shown in Figure 5.3.

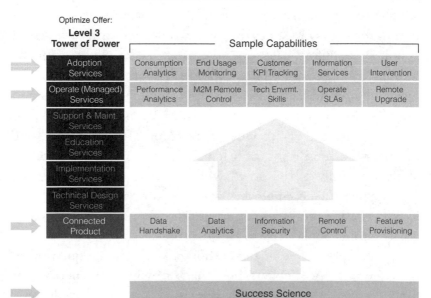

FIGURE 5.3 Sample Product and Service Capabilities at Level 3 in the Tower of Power

Two are new service offers—remote operate services (commonly called managed services) and the all-new notion of adoption services. The third—connected product—may or may not be a separate offer, but it is an essential capability. But where we really want to start our discussion is with the underlying foundation for the Tower of Power—a knowledge capability that will empower nearly every floor in the structure.

Success Science

Last year we had an epiphany, at least for us. We were leading a roundtable discussion at the spring 2012 Technology Services World conference. It was a session that was not on the published agenda and was for invited guests only. Around the table were senior service executives from 40 of the world's largest high-tech companies. The topic was the changing nature of service employee skills needed by tech suppliers as we move into the era of consumption economics. It was a hard conversation. We were talking about many jobs, many great employees, many years of dedication to the tech companies they worked for, and many wonderful people who, unfortunately, may lack the needed skill sets for the future. But we pressed forward, talking about the shifts from technical skills toward business skills, from troubleshooting software to troubleshooting business processes, from service employees who head right for the device when they go onto the customer's site to ones who head right for a senior customer executive's office. When we really boiled down what we were saying, it was that tech suppliers need employees who could find out what "right" looked like for the customer, not those who could troubleshoot what "wrong" looked like with the product.

At one point, one of the authors asked a simple question of the attendees: "As suppliers, how many of you have a permanent function at your company—a team of people who study how your most successful customers became your most successful customers?" Guess what the answer was? None. We all—every one of us in the room at that moment—knew immediately that this was not good. "How can that be?" we asked rhetorically. Then, as if out of the mouths of babes, we said it: "Don't we need to be studying that? Don't we need some kind of . . . ah . . . er . . . Success Science?" And there it was: Success Science—the study of the science behind customer success. There were a lot of shaking heads in the room. Only one company out of the 40 present said it had a capability within its company that was even remotely close. Sure everyone had product developers or product marketing managers who were trying to figure out which features customers wanted so the company could make its products sell better, but no one was really trying formally to sort out all of the best practices of customers who took that functionality and escorted it all the way through to optimized business outcomes. That sounded like a worthy goal, like a business capability that most suppliers were going to need in the new world of consumption economics.

In the months after that meeting, we reflected on why such a critical supplier capability could have escaped becoming mainstream at so many companies for so long? After all, IBM was producing best-practice documents called IBM Redbooks back in the 1970s. We think the answer goes back to the same point we have made over and over again: For some strange reason, in the old B2B partnership model, suppliers were allowed to stay close to their products while customers willingly assumed the responsibility for their outcomes. That the customer was an "*n* of 1" while the supplier could have had visibility across an "*n* of many" customers did not seem to matter. As we pointed out, the supplier was paid up front, signed the customer onto a long-term maintenance contract, and then turned the focus of the sales and technical team who won this deal onto winning the next one.

Beginning at Level 3, that operating model is no longer sufficient. Even the Redbooks are not enough. Once suppliers' revenue is tied to usage levels, or even to the outcomes that the customer achieves, they will want to get into the game side by side with the customer. The question is, doing what? What are the key activities that suppliers want to partner with customers to achieve? This is precisely what Success Science tries to isolate.

Success Science is best defined as a constant process—not a one-time project—that synthesizes multiple data and information inputs in a structured manner to articulate a solution's key success factors and the best practices to achieve them. Once understood, a supplier can use it to reproduce those conditions in as many customer sites as possible.

With the shift to XaaS (even without it!), suppliers need to start with a better understanding of who their most successful customers are. Even that turns out to be a more hotly debated topic than you might think. Only by doing so can they then begin to study them and design a clear path to creating multiple high-value, high-consuming customers. In Chapter 7, we will talk about the new, more risky breakeven profile that suppliers take on in XaaS deals. Their profits will no longer be locked in once the up-front contract is signed. They will only make money if the customer is a high-consuming one. For that reason alone, Success Science is going to be huge. That is why we are working closely with our friends on the consulting side of PwC not only to define its key attributes, but also to understand exactly what science should be brought to bear.

As a simple example, let's take salesforce.com. It has thousands of sales forces using its product to keep track of forecasts. Those customers are probably using dozens, if not hundreds, of different sales forecasting methods. So does salesforce.com know which of these methods yields the most accurate 30-, 60-, and 90-day forecasts? They should! Does salesforce.com know which one works best in a supplies business versus a capital equipment business? They could. Would all of salesforce.com's customers like to know exactly which sales forecasting method is going to work best for them? You bet. And would customers like to know that up front, and not after years of trial and error using spreadsheets outside their expensive customer relationship management (CRM) system? We believe so.

Success Science could be a new department on its own, or simply a new function performed by an existing department within the supplier. Importantly, its job is not to "own" the customer. We think the best analogy is that the Success Science process creates the sheet music that the supplier's orchestra of sales, service, and other supporting functions will follow to ensure optimal customer outcomes. That means the Success Science team will work with both customers and employees to do things such as the following:

- Maintain a library of successful technical architectures that technical solution architects can draw from.

- Identify the deployment plans that customers have been most successful with for various combinations of products.

- Identify the KPIs that are the important determinants of customer success in the supplier's key markets. Specify for R&D the data streams and analytics required in the products to monitor those KPIs.

- Identify best customer business processes for critical areas of product utilization.

- Analyze the high-performing customers in key markets to define what key features, and in what order, various end users must perfect in order to optimize their job role outcomes.

- Develop and keep current the skill requirement profiles that various departments of the supplier and the customer need to have available within their workforces.

These are but a few of the many things that the Success Science team must do to harness the power of the "n of many" experts and data sources that can be found within a particular supplier's ecosystem. To deliver on its potential, the teams will need to analyze the sales and service histories of successful customers. They will need to visit them, observe them, and question them. They will need to collect "big data" about product usage and analyze patterns. They will need a structured process for interviewing employees and resellers to see what they have learned while working with multiple customers.

Great Success Science practitioners will not only study their customers and interview their employees; they will also need to constantly scan the horizon for new ideas and capabilities to increase success rates. This means not only studying competitive suppliers, but also keeping one's "head up" regarding the worlds of B2B and B2C. These are costly endeavors, especially when done right. They are akin to many of the "Big M" marketing processes of B2C companies that we described in Chapter 2. But they are going to be more than nice things to know; they are going to become keys to the profitability and differentiation of the B4B supplier and to the success of its customers. To put it bluntly, we don't think customer satisfaction surveys and loyalty indexes are good enough to capture the voice of the customer. Beginning at Level 3, suppliers need to lead the customer to success, not track whether it happened after the fact. Success Science is the key capability that they need.

Outcome Services

Success Science is the foundational capability of the Tower of Power. It represents the supplier's ability to harness the power of its ecosystem's "*n* of many" experiences. On top of that solid foundation, we can build the floors of the tower. The new "floors" in the Level 3 and Level 4 towers are a set of services that we refer to as optimize and outcome services (see Figure 5.4). The primary mission of these services is to bring the power from the library of Success Science capabilities to bear on a single business customer.

The backdrop for these services is a story familiar to nearly everyone. In high-tech and complex near-tech industries, it has been easy for customers to fall into the trap of focusing heavily on the challenges of getting a new piece of technology operational. The huge complexities of installation, integration, testing, commissioning,

Optimize and Outcome Services

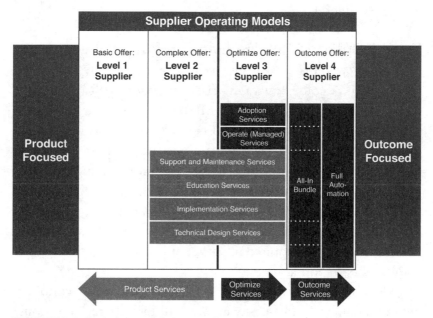

FIGURE 5.4 Optimize and Outcome Services

training, and so on could be all-consuming for both the customer and the supplier. In fact, they often consumed *all* the hours that the customer could afford to dedicate or purchase for the project. The result was a practice that often proved unproductive: Implement first; optimize later. The thinking was that once the massive technical obstacles were overcome, the customer could begin focusing on the keys to optimal utilization. But too often, that second step didn't take place with the same dedication and commitment to resources as the first; sometimes it didn't happen at all. When that step fails to be taken seriously, adoption lags. Users may find alternatives or cling to their old manual ways. The result was often that the customer executives were forced to accept an investment whose business outcomes were less than hoped for. It is also why suppliers can install exactly the same product for two similar customers and have them deliver two completely different results.

Beginning at Level 3, optimize services are there to put an end to that story. Their mission is to ensure that each customer gets value rapidly, achieves the highest ROI, and does so with the lowest possible TCO.

Level 3 Optimize Service Lines and Capabilities

At Level 3, we think the already hot market for operate (managed) services will be joined by a new class of services we call adoption services. Let's start with the former because it is so well known.

Operate or Managed Services is often defined as the outsourcing of day-to-day IT management responsibilities as a strategic method for improving the operations of high-tech or near-tech products and systems. A decade ago, this offer was full of friction and labor. Today, the cloud version of managed services offers the ability to remotely perform many valuable tasks. Many new capabilities are required if a supplier is to be successful. We list a few examples in Figure 5.5.

Managed services can help operate some or all of a technology environment. The tasks performed could include remote monitoring, system management, network management, performance

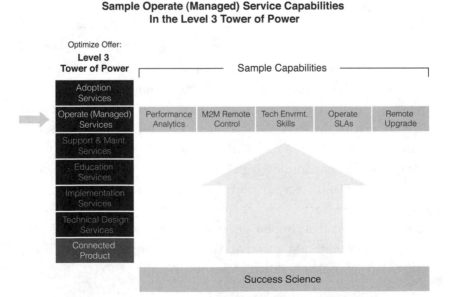

FIGURE 5.5 Sample Operate (Managed) Service Capabilities in the Tower of Power at Level 3

optimization, data management, or hosting. The result is better system performance at lower cost. Depending on the customer requirement and the technical capability of the supplier, the blend of on-site versus remote labor and automated cloud services will differ. TSIA has outstanding best-practice research on how a supplier should structure and optimize their managed service line.

Adoption services is a new idea, at least as a formal service line. But we think these services are going to be a huge new advancement for suppliers and customers.

These services will seek to plan, monitor, accelerate, and optimize the adoption of product capability by users and/or other systems. Adoption services might work closely with the technical solutions architect to build a plan to develop the complete business solution, to smooth the edges of complexity on both sides, and to make the outcome more frictionless. Rather than "implement first; optimize later," the customer and the supplier can work on both concurrently. But once again, the supplier must acquire new capabilities. Figure 5.6 shows a few examples.

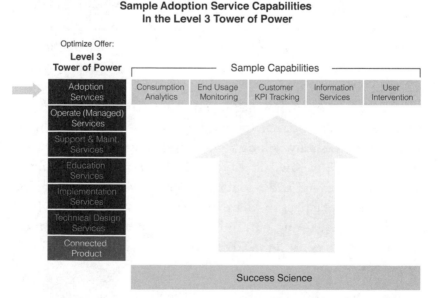

FIGURE 5.6 Sample Adoption Service Capabilities in the Tower of Power at Level 3

The most basic, but perhaps most popular, adoption services offer may simply be consumption monitoring and reporting: The ability to report to a business customer's senior executives how well a product or system is being utilized by their employees is a breakthrough unto itself. But more powerfully, adoption services will aid in the success rate of end users. It could promote first-time feature use or could remediate repeated-failure feature use. They might accomplish that through "in-use" chat, the "just-in-time" delivery of targeted video, or other content through the product interface—even YouTube tutorials that are delivered to smartphones so users can learn key features "on the go." Next, imagine a remote "do-it-for-me" capability or an on-demand feature provision that both improves user productivity for the customer and increases billable consumption for the supplier. It might also improve the information within a product or a system, maybe through the supplier or through third-party data sources in the ecosystem. In the case of industrial equipment, examples might include improving data exchanges between systems, data cleaning, or remote operation of complex features. Examples of important underlying capabilities include robust consumption analytics, flexible KPI monitoring, in-use education content for end-user intervention, and data/information enhancement. We cover adoption services in more depth in Chapter 8.

These services represent powerful opportunities for Level 3 suppliers to help optimize the ROI of business customers. Building them successfully will be a multi-year journey for every supplier. At TSIA, we are identifying all the necessary capabilities to deliver managed and adoption services. We are then linking industry best practices to them. We believe that they can be built on top of the existing customer service infrastructure of most Level 2 suppliers. In a world in which it is *and*, not *or*, this is important.

Product Capabilities That Enable Optimize Services

These new service offers are going to be a beautiful thing for customers. However, in order to be just as beautiful for suppliers, they need to be made highly scalable and relatively frictionless. This will only be achieved if the right capabilities have been engineered into the product, as shown in Figure 5.7.

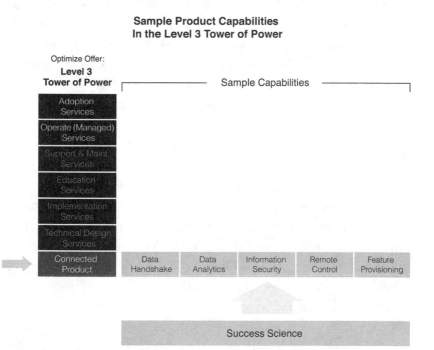

FIGURE 5.7 Sample Product Capabilities in the Tower of Power at Level 3

As we have said repeatedly, Level 3 suppliers must work out their "data handshake" with customers. We cover this more completely in Chapter 9. Once the data is available, the supplier must have the capability to analyze it effectively and link the findings to the service layers up higher in the tower. We discuss some of these important new analytics capabilities in more detail in Chapter 8.

Another example of a new product capability is the ability to remotely control the product and intervene with its end users. Although many suppliers can do some of this to some degree today, we are thinking of a much more robust version, something more akin to what B2C companies have learned to do. Not only can B2C suppliers intervene to suggest consumers back up their data; they can also perform that work for them. Not only can B2C e-commerce suppliers offer a HELP button at the top of the page; they can also pop up chat windows when consumers fail to check out their shopping cart. B2C suppliers have learned to both remotely control their products and to intervene directly with end users in the course of actually using them. Soon they will do it with live video connections. This is one of those areas in which B2C companies lead and B2B companies should follow.

A third key technical capability is what we call controllable feature provisioning: the ability to have product functionality "unfold" to an end user, a system administrator, or a plant floor operator as needed. Specific examples could include the capability to turn features on or off based on job-role priorities, process requirements, customer-determined priorities, or demonstrated mastery/high utilization of existing functions of the product. This capability is frequently seen in consumer gaming applications through which end users, based on their scores at more basic levels, see more advanced weapons and competitors. It is effectively how Apple manages the usage complexity of iPhones by giving end users the ability to add and remove apps at will. By simplifying feature sets in a smart way, you both accelerate basic adoption as well as dramatically improve the odds of moving users up to more powerful capabilities. If they have trouble along the way, we can now intervene directly through the product to assist them.

We think that these four elements of the Level 3 Tower of Power—Success Science, connected products, operate (managed) services, and adoption services—are going to be essential for success. Returning to our car engine metaphor, the result will not only be a new, more powerful engine, but one that requires new organizational capabilities to fuel it.

Level 4 Outcome Service Lines

As we mentioned in the last chapter, many product companies are or may soon surprise themselves by playing at Level 4, as shown in Figure 5.8.

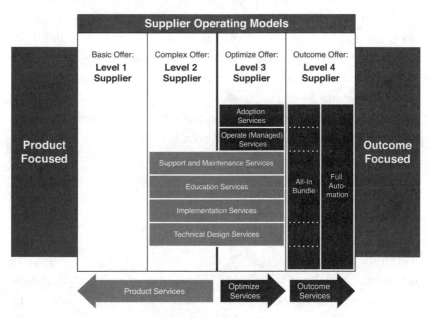

Optimize and Outcome Services

	Supplier Operating Models			
	Basic Offer: **Level 1 Supplier**	Complex Offer: **Level 2 Supplier**	Optimize Offer: **Level 3 Supplier**	Outcome Offer: **Level 4 Supplier**

Product Focused

Adoption Services

Operate (Managed) Services

Support and Maintenance Services

Education Services

Implementation Services

Technical Design Services

All-In Bundle

Full Auto-mation

Outcome Focused

Product Services → Optimize Services → Outcome Services

FIGURE 5.8 Optimize and Outcome Services

They may do so because their largest customers ask them to. Or maybe it will be because they are paid *only* if the outcome is realized, such as in true consumption pricing, revenue sharing, or gain sharing. And finally, they may play at Level 4 because they have amassed so much technology and so many skills in a particular area that they can fully automate a solution to enable a customer to get a game-changing result simply by plugging in. In any case, it means they are willing to warrant that they have mastered their domain and its complexity. As we said in the last chapter, Level 4 can be both glamorous and dangerous. With tons of experimentation and risk taking going on, this is also the most fluid of the four supplier levels.

Because we have already described the process of attaching capabilities to the offers in the Level 3 tower, we won't repeat the exercise for Level 4. We will just provide some additional thoughts and offer a few examples of both Level 4 offers.

All-in bundles are tempting to offer and the most dangerous to attempt. These bundles represent the end of the road for many component-level tech offers. It is the ultimate bundle: EaaS (everything as a service). That means the Level 4 supplier has so much confidence in their understanding of how to get a successful customer outcome that they will charge only for the platform's actual results. Under the covers of this offer, inside their Tower of Power engines, suppliers may still rely on classic product and service components and capabilities, but they are not ones for which the customer pays separately. Customers just pay for the experience: The supplier absorbs any complexities and risk. An all-in bundle is perfect for catering to very large customers who want to turn over parts of their operation to a product supplier. More and more large customers are asking for that. More large suppliers are carefully sticking their toes into the water as a result. If you are a wireless carrier, maybe a product company will build and operate your 4G network and then share in the monthly revenue from each subscriber. IBM's Smarter Planet activities could also fit here. By developing new platform services to help cities manage traffic or to help power companies build smart utility grids, IBM not only differentiates using a Level 4 approach; it also helps pull many of its Level 2 and Level 3 offers. You can also bet that Xerox is hard at work trying to turn ACS's management of the New York State electronic toll road system into a reusable platform that other transportation agencies will want. We think that what is essential to the success of all-in bundles is to negotiate a true shift of control over how the domain is operated. If the Level 4 supplier has the responsibility but the customer is still in control of deciding how it will work, the project will fail and both parties will lose. The supplier must prove that it has mastered the domain, and the customer must be willing to acquiesce control in exchange for a lower-risk, less-complex variable pricing model.

Full automation is the true utility model that has been talked about for years. It is the glamorous model of new start-ups and it certainly is an attractive one for customers. As we have said, this is where suppliers such as Amazon Web Services and Rackspace are heading. In their pure retail form, they will often be another form of "all in" offer through which additional service fees are usually not charged. Although glamorous, this true utility model has not yet proved itself to be dependably profitable or free from commoditization in the long term. For these reasons, we think the defining characteristic of a successful Level 4 full automation offer is that suppliers will have truly succeeded at engineering out all of the complexity for customers. They have mastered it to the point that not only has software eaten all the old product and service components that existed at Levels 2 and 3, but the software is also elegantly simple and requires very little labor from either side. The Tower of Power at this level must also have incredible analytic and automated intervention capability. A full automation offer is the perfect supplier strategy when low prices and high volume can disrupt a market full of expensive Level 2 or Level 3 competitors.

The use of Level 4 offers can vary widely. Some suppliers will compete in large, well-known markets like offering parts of a data center in the cloud. But there will be many variations on Level 4 strategies, and not all will be "public" offers. Maybe a product company has built a highly useful technology wrapper around their Level 2 or Level 3 products that can improve their existing customers' outcomes. Maybe some enterprising engineers have built a technology platform that can connect multiple customers of a single supplier together to share knowledge or even share custom software. Perhaps that supplier's customers could join together on the platform to create a buying group to cut their supply chain costs. Maybe the supplier offers a technology platform that different business customers can access on a white-label basis, add their logo, and then bring it to market under their own brand. A good example of this might be to provide a platform allowing a business customer to build and manage a third-party apps community. To qualify as a Level 4 offer, it must be a reusable platform but does not need to be available on the open market. The suppliers can target it to as few or as many customers as they want.

The Tower of Power Is the Equivalent of the B2C Platform of Service

Starting at Level 3 and continuing to Level 4, the B4B Tower of Power is a stack of technology-fueled, data-driven capabilities. These capabilities are the beginnings of the complete service experience platform we described innovative B2C and (a few) B2B companies using in Chapter 2. Those companies rely on that platform to deliver a great customer outcome that will, in turn, sell more products. There is near certainty that it will make its way into the mainstream of B4B within the next decade. Many of the individual underlying capabilities already exist, and most every one is being delivered somewhere by someone today. What has not happened in B2B so far is one supplier putting it all together—becoming the Frankenstein that we think is now possible. No two will look exactly alike. Suppliers must design their own Tower of Power just as Amazon, Rackspace, Apple, and salesforce.com are well on their way to doing. Each day, they get farther ahead of companies that have not yet begun the journey. Taken all together, the Tower of Power (or some variation of it) will become the backbone of Level 3 and Level 4 suppliers. It allows these suppliers to build outcome-driven operating models—ones that can play a constant, high-value role in their partnership with customers and do so with the scalability they crave.

But in order for a supplier to become truly outcome-driven, as we have mentioned many times, a big shift in management thinking, for *both* suppliers and their customers, is required. Neither is really used to the supplier being in that role.

This made us wonder: Where else in the economy are suppliers really outcome-driven? In searching for that answer, we ran across an analogy that you might resist at first but grow to appreciate the more you think about it.

Just What the Doctor Ordered

One complex industry in which suppliers are very focused on achieving great outcomes for their customers is health care. And one of the best at being outcome-driven is the Cleveland Clinic. So much so that *Forbes* magazine singled it out as somewhere businesses should look to for inspiration.

Figure 5.9 tells a pretty amazing story. It considers both patient volumes (in this case, for cardiac surgery) and something called the "mortality index." In 2011, compared to six other top US hospitals, the Cleveland Clinic had *both* the highest patient volume and the lowest mortality index. This is an impressive

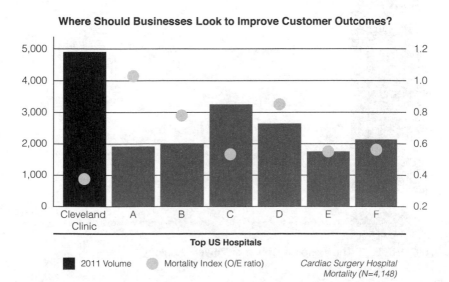

FIGURE 5.9 Where Should Businesses Look to Improve Customer Outcomes?

result. For the Cleveland Clinic, quality and volume are clearly not opposing forces. It has found ways to ensure great customer (patient) outcomes at very high volume levels on a very complex offer. *Forbes* calls them both a "well-oiled machine" as well as an "economic bright spot."[4]

Running across this article made us wonder what top hospitals have learned about being outcome-driven organizations. The more looking we did, the more we saw the parallels between how hospitals function and the Tower of Power construct. (Now before you ask yourself, "Aren't most hospitals losing money? Why would I want to emulate them?" consider that they are fighting market dynamics that few B2B suppliers face. Besides, it doesn't change the fact that they are masters of outcome management.) Start reading at the bottom of the chart shown in Figure 5.10. They are all experiences you have witnessed. Just look at how analogous their operating model is!

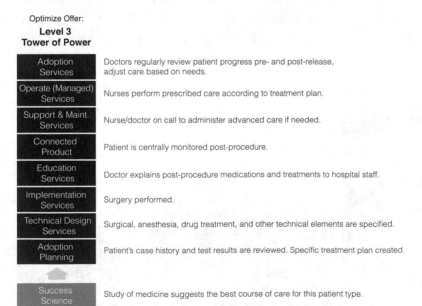

FIGURE 5.10 The Hospital "Tower of Power" Analogy

Importantly, at the foundation of the hospital's tower is the huge base of scientific research on causes, treatments, and outcomes that have been conducted in the study of medicine. This body of work, the health care version of Success Science, informs and shapes practically every other layer in the operating model. By reading up from the bottom and noting the analogous Level 3 Tower of Power activity to the left, you can see how an industry that has spent centuries focused on optimizing customer outcomes uses many of the general principles that we anticipate seeing in B4B operating models.

What Does It Mean to You?

So if you are a high-tech or near-tech supplier, the key questions we would ask you are these: What will *your* Tower of Power look like? Can you erase our generic names in the rectangles and assign your real ones? Can you list the new organizational capabilities you will need to develop? Can you identify the existing organizations or teams that would take the lead in these new roles? Without a Tower of Power and the right underlying capabilities, you will not be able to play at Levels 3 and 4. It will simply be cost prohibitive: too much friction and too much labor. Try drawing your own Tower of Power. What percentage of your tower already exists? How long will it take for you to fill in the blanks?

If you are a business customer, here is what we would ask you to ponder: How ready, willing, and able you are to connect to Level 3 and Level 4 suppliers? In what parts of the business are you willing to pilot these new operating models? Are there certain applications or production capabilities where these kinds of partnerships would be particularly well suited? Are there others that scare you? You should be sorting those answers out internally. Try to decide where your first Level 3 "beta test" might be. You can even use the B4B model to start defining the RFP attributes you may look for in your potential beta partners.

Let's end this chapter by recalling a semi-famous quote. Nicholas Negroponte, founder of the Massachusetts Institute of Technology (MIT) Media Lab, once made the pithy observation that "the Internet was the most overhyped, underestimated phenomenon in history." We think the same thing about some of today's cloud business models. We think that, in 2013, XaaS is overhyped and underestimated. The hype is too focused on hosting and pricing. We think connectedness and the Tower of Power are going to be the things that have the most lasting impact on the value that business customers achieve through technology. The potential long-term impact of the Level 3 and Level 4 supplier models is only now coming into view. We can't promise that every supplier will be able to guarantee every customer outcome, but what we can say is that having them on the playing field as part of the customer's outcome team is guaranteed to put points on the scoreboard.

The next question, especially for Level 2 suppliers, is how to get there from where they are today.

6 | Capabilities-Led Transformation

Because we believe the supplier's operating model is the key lever in improving customer outcomes, we will start the "how" conversation from the supplier side. Let's begin that discussion by touching on an experience familiar to many Level 1 and Level 2 suppliers. It is one that we think can be very instructional as a reference point—a reference point for both what *to do* and what *not to do* in any upcoming transformation.

Suppliers have long known that a great way to increase the market penetration and/or extend the life of a product or core technology is to segment the market and develop targeted offerings. In the world of software, this was most often accomplished through vertical market versions of the product. For example, by building in key features that the banking industry or the insurance industry needed most, suppliers could reduce the need for customers to customize their generic, cross-market product. That made the offer easier and more practical for companies in those vertical markets to purchase. In hardware or industrial equipment, the niche game was often about finding specific markets that needed specialized versions of the core technology. Sometimes it meant special housing that accommodated a rugged environment. Other times it meant developing special-purpose variants on the product for industries such as health care or process manufacturing. These techniques for increasing market adoption or extending product lives are hardly new. Manufacturers and software companies have used them successfully for decades.

Two lessons from this experience are relevant to our conversation: First, it works. Second, it has an impact on a supplier's cost structure. As we have often said, suppliers prefer to stay close to their product. In a perfect world, it would be a standard, generic product with broad cross-market appeal. For suppliers, this is usually the optimal profit model—one that allows them to achieve maximum scale with minimal friction. The minute they start down the path of developing niche versions of their cross-market product, they have to start focusing on more than one target audience. They now need multiple iterations of that product, increasing their development and manufacturing costs. They may need new knowledge in the sales force or a different reseller channel. They may have to start unique marketing campaigns for each target niche. In short, they have to focus on the different needs of multiple sets of customers, not just one. Historically, this multi-market focus has led to some redundancy of effort, even to parallel organizations within the same supplier. In some cases, it has actually triggered huge reorganizations by suppliers: They slice up the different functions such as R&D, sales, and service into separate market-specific teams and then stitch them back together vertically into what management believes will be more nimble, market-focused business units. They are almost like companies within the company.

We fully understand why B2B suppliers often reach the conclusion that successful focus requires dedicated organizations. In traditional B2B, we support that it was often the right decision. But we question whether it is the right approach in B4B.

This is because we think the need for "focus areas" is going to increase exponentially. If every new focus area means a new organization (what we will refer to as focus = organization), suppliers' cost structures will soon spiral out of control. In many high-tech and near-tech markets in which product prices and margins are falling, this seems like a recipe for disaster. Instead, we think suppliers need to increase the aptitude of their core organizations to be capable of multiple focus areas at once. Only then can they retain the economies of scale that will be so important to future profitability. We realize that this is a huge challenge, one that many smart companies have already tried to conquer to little avail. In fact, we think it has been a major reason why the early pioneers of operating model transformation have struggled to achieve the level of success they had hoped for.

Early Efforts to Transform

There have already been a number of interesting attempts to transform from a Level 2 supplier into something that has a similar shape and form to Level 3 and 4 of B4B. We can identify at least three approaches that companies have taken to get there, as shown in Figure 6.1. These represent different paths to managing the introduction of a new model to the large, established core operating model of a supplier.

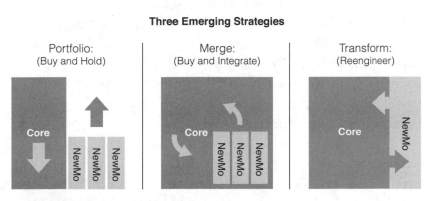

FIGURE 6.1 Three Emerging Strategies

Let's discuss these from left to right because, so far, most of the attempts to transform Level 2 suppliers have been made by acquiring new model (NewMo) companies.

In 2008, HP bought EDS. In HP's press release, then–CEO Mark Hurd said, "This reinforces our commitment to help customers manage and transform their technology to achieve better results."[1] Sound familiar? It did not take long before others got into the transformation game through acquisition. Just one year later, in 2009, Xerox bought outsourcer ACS (Affiliated Computer Services) for $6.4 billion. In the Xerox press release, CEO Ursula Burns said, "By combining Xerox's strengths in document technology with ACS's expertise in managing and automating work processes, we're creating a new class of solution provider."[2] Sound like a Level 2 supplier buying its way into Level 3? That same year, Dell spent $3.9 billion to acquire Perot Systems with much the same storyline (great tech products company buys great tech services company to create great new outcome-focused company).

All of these were examples of hardware companies trying to guard against commoditization at Level 2 by moving to a new model that they hoped would create differentiation, value, and profitable growth—just like it had for IBM. EDS, ACS, and Perot were often referred to as outsourcers in those days, but what they all had in common was an operating model that tied them closer to their business customers' actual outcomes. They didn't just sell them products. They also tried to help operate the products. They tried to help drive better outcomes. They tried to be game changers. Clearly the intent of the CEOs of HP, Xerox, and Dell (using our language) was to transform parts of the parent companies from being Level 2 complex offer suppliers into being Level 3 and Level 4 outcome suppliers.

There was also a wave of movement in software, storage, and network markets. Once SaaS established itself as a viable and disruptive business model, several large Level 2 suppliers began buying the NewMo provocateurs. Cisco bought WebEx in 2007. In 2011, traditional software giants like Oracle and SAP led an army of companies eager to gobble up interesting NewMo companies such as Taleo, RightNow, and SuccessFactors. To compete with

AWS, EMC formed Pivotal from its Greenplum acquisition in 2013. It was a different cast of characters acting out the same storyline: traditionally profitable Level 2 companies furiously moving into high-growth, new model spaces.

We worked with the big hardware companies before and after their 2008/2009 acquisitions. In the software wave, we had front-row seats to the action. We had worked with the big companies, we had worked with most of the pre-acquisition SaaS companies, and then we worked with the combined entities. In looking across them, two classic acquisition integration patterns can be seen. The first is the portfolio strategy, shown in Figure 6.2.

Strategy One:
Portfolio—Buy and Hold

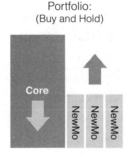

Portfolio:
(Buy and Hold)

Idea: Buy emerging NewMo leaders in your space. Leave them free to continue to share gains without interruption. Let core business stand as long as possible. Leave future options for integration open.

Plus: Both Core and NewMo are left to do what they do best. Strategy defends the category against new competitors and captures upside potential. Core can introduce NewMo to more customers. Easiest strategy to execute.

Minus: Core never transforms, or transforms too late. Core erodes quickly—looks old. NewMos don't benefit from scale of Core, do not materialize at expected profitability, or develop with price points not assumable by Core. Can end up with duplicate cost structures.

FIGURE 6.2 Strategy One: Portfolio—Buy and Hold

You might look at this as a way to place smart bets on the future. Large Level 2 suppliers took advantage of their big balance sheets and large market caps to buy upstart, NewMo companies that were either competitive or complementary. This strategy has many potential benefits. The first is defensive. They buy the right to eliminate the NewMo company as a competitor. Second, they buy growth. This strategy is both easy to understand and relatively easy to execute. In particular, if you got these companies early enough when the price was reasonable, it made a lot of sense.

If you waited too long, they could become quite pricey—for example, Oracle's buying salesforce.com today rather than in 2004.

The problem with the portfolio strategy is that it rarely transforms the core of the new parent. Since most large suppliers think that focus = organization, they leave the acquisition's organization separate to "do its thing." The attributes that made the NewMo successful sit ensconced in their shell. The core hopes that NewMo will grow big enough and fast enough to someday be a meaningful contributor to the core's income statement. Large suppliers often place multiple bets by buying a number of NewMo companies that may have this potential. Perhaps one acquisition's "thing" could even grow large enough to become the new core. But so far, that has rarely happened. EMC's acquisition of VMware has been a great success, but it still sits mostly separate from EMC's core. EMC seems to have organized Pivotal in a similar manner, as a separate brand and as a mostly separate organization. Fortunately for EMC, its core is still profitable and modestly growing, so it retains the option of merging the portfolio later. For other suppliers, their cores may already have begun deteriorating. They may need to move faster in their transformation efforts.

Although we have not really counted hands, we would guess the portfolio strategy is the favorite of Level 2 supplier CEOs, especially ones who believe that focus = organization. It is both defensively and offensively advantageous, and it requires "only" cash or stock, not gut-wrenching organizational transformation.

The second strategy is to merge. We think the merge strategy, so far, has the best potential and the worst results. You can see the potential for problems just by looking at Figure 6.3.

What happens is that the massive weight of the core can easily crush the innovation of the NewMo company. The crushing is not intentional. The logic is that the core is a massive, experienced giant compared to the cute, naïve upstart. The core wants to help "mature it," to put it on the big-time Level 2 platform. Doing this misses the point. Just as the B2C companies have become the

Strategy Two:
Merge—Buy and Integrate

Merge:
(Buy and Integrate)

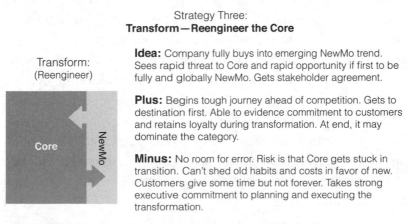

Idea: Buy emerging NewMo leaders in your space. Integrate them into Core. Let innovative models and capabilities slowly permeate and transform the Core both in the offers and in the delivery. Leverage the scale of the Core to accelerate the NewMo.

Plus: NewMo grows faster and Core begins to learn the lessons.

Minus: Core eats the NewMo. NewMo is too little to compete for internal resources and Core is too set in its ways to transform. Core gets distracted and NewMo is never heard from again. Takes strong executive commitment to the NewMos.

FIGURE 6.3 Strategy Two: Merge—Buy and Integrate

teachers, the Level 3 XaaS companies often have much to teach their new owners. But so far, they have struggled to get to the chalkboard.

The strategy that seems the most difficult (and the least attempted) is transforming the core (see Figure 6.4).

Strategy Three:
Transform—Reengineer the Core

Transform:
(Reengineer)

Idea: Company fully buys into emerging NewMo trend. Sees rapid threat to Core and rapid opportunity if first to be fully and globally NewMo. Gets stakeholder agreement.

Plus: Begins tough journey ahead of competition. Gets to destination first. Able to evidence commitment to customers and retains loyalty during transformation. At end, it may dominate the category.

Minus: No room for error. Risk is that Core gets stuck in transition. Can't shed old habits and costs in favor of new. Customers give some time but not forever. Takes strong executive commitment to planning and executing the transformation.

FIGURE 6.4 Strategy Three: Transform—Reengineer the Core

We would argue that the main obstacle to transforming the core is simultaneously achieving multiple focus areas. The difficulty of teaching the old dog new tricks in the past has led many executives to conclude that a new focus area can only be successful if a separate organization is established. Let us give you a real-world example of this belief that is being played out all over the high-tech industry right now: the building of new managed services organizations.

TSIA data clearly show that the fastest growing of all high-tech service lines is managed services. The cloud and connected products have enabled some suppliers to take over many system management tasks that their business customers used to do internally. Because they have better tools to automate those chores and because they can use those tools to serve many customers at a time, they can offer lower prices and sometimes better performance than the old in-house alternative. As we said in Chapter 4, it makes sense, and the market is responding positively.

Inside many large Level 2 high-tech suppliers today, there is a turf war going on over who gets to run the managed services business. The executives who run the professional services organization think they should own it. The executives who run the customer service and support organization think they should own it. Both can build a great case for why they are the best choice. Know who's winning? Neither. In most companies today, cloud-based managed services are being established as a separate organization. So now there aren't just four commonly distinct service organizations in high-tech; there are five. When adoption services become reality, there could be six. And if the supplier moves to Level 4, there could be seven or eight.

We don't think this model works. This is not teaching the old dog new tricks; it is just adding more dogs. This doesn't transform the core; it simply enlarges it, one organization on top of another on top of another.

Merging Capabilities

Of the three transformation strategies that large suppliers have been using, we like the merge, but not necessarily the way it has been done so far. We think most Level 2 suppliers have been buying organizations when what they should be buying is capabilities.

The concept of capabilities in business is certainly nothing new. In the last chapter, we provided the definition we use at TSIA: Capabilities represent the organizational ability to achieve desired results. They could be processes, skills, metrics, or technologies. We view capabilities as the building blocks of a company's operating model—for both suppliers and customers. We think they will achieve a whole new level of significance in B4B. Quite simply, the potential to do new things, achieve new results, supplant labor, and increase reaction times today is unparalleled. There has never been "connectedness" with business customers like this before, there has never been the potential for a Tower of Power at Level 3, and there has never been the ability to let data and analytics drive organizational reactions with such precision and scale. We have actually applied this approach to our research on well-run service organizations. We have identified the specific component capabilities that support services, field services, professional services, education services, and managed services organizations need to be successful. Now that we have identified them, we are going one step further, seeking out the industry's best practices for each of these capabilities from across our 300 member companies. It is becoming a fact-based set of building blocks for how to make a tech service business remarkable. This is why we think—in fact, we know—that suppliers can now build their core organizations to handle many focus areas simultaneously.

We were talking about this using Amazon's consumer e-commerce business as a simple example. Amazon started by selling books. It built an e-commerce platform to do so. Then it moved into other markets such as consumer electronics, apparel, and eventually lab equipment and industrial supplies. Imagine if Amazon had taken the route of focus = organization when it came to its platform! There might not be one Amazon.com platform; there might have been 20. Instead, it focused its resources on building a single, dynamic platform with diverse capabilities. That one website keeps adding new capabilities when new product lines require them. But for any one customer who is shopping for one thing, all he or she sees is the relevant platform capabilities. When you are buying clothes, you can look at them in different colors with one click, but not when you are buying books or TVs. By taking this approach, Amazon gained the growth benefits of diversifying into many market segments without compromising scalability. They appear to be taking that same approach with Amazon Web Services. While it does appear to have built a second platform for AWS, Amazon is expanding this platform into multiple new business computing markets without creating redundancy. Although we realize that there is a big difference between giving technology platforms new capabilities and giving organizations new capabilities, we think the example is instructive.

We are promoting the same concept to the thousands of senior technology service executives who are part of the TSIA communities in IT, health care, industrial equipment, and consumer technology. Each year we study how tech companies organize their service businesses. As we've mentioned, there are usually between three and six separate service organizations at most high-tech and near-tech companies. These suppliers have typically organized their services according to the focus = organization model by making each service line its own organization. We also study which functions within these organizations are globally managed and which are out in the field, reporting to geo leaders.

Rather than adding new service organizations, we recommend learning new tricks. We are working with members to develop a model for converged services. The critical concept behind converged services is "organizational capabilities." In this model, some capabilities are shared among service lines while other capabilities are unique to specific service lines. We call for more investment in shared capabilities like service engineering, practice design, technology infrastructure, and knowledge management that are globally managed across all service lines. We also see more virtual teaming across service lines to help meet a large customer's specific needs. We call for an increase in remote and a decrease in on-site service labor—again leaning toward more global management. Not everyone is happy about our stance. It means some independent fiefdoms may be less independent. But we think that this will be the trend in the industry—one with many financial and quality advantages. You can read more about Services Convergence principles in *Complexity Avalanche*[3] or about current best practices at TSIA. But what it goes to prove is that we are on the cusp of decoupling the notion that focus must = organization, at least in services.

Earlier we said that we think the need for "focus areas" is going to increase exponentially in B4B. The mathematical permutations are intimidating. Take almost any supplier and multiply the number of products it offers by the unique markets it serves. Many will require more than one operating model. This could result in dozens or even hundreds of focus areas. Each one simply cannot be its own organization! Not even most of them can be. We need a more flexible core, not the Byzantine Empire.

To accomplish this, we suggest that they think as a flexible discrete manufacturer would. These companies procure different manufacturing capabilities that enable them to build different kinds of discrete products. Based on what their customers need them to manufacture, they can string those capabilities together in different ways: They can build to order. All they need is a work order, a design spec, and a bill of materials (BOM). They don't build a separate factory for each production run; they use or don't use certain manufacturing capabilities that they have procured over time. Certain new capabilities allow them to get into new markets. When they decide to enter a new market, the factory managers identify and add any missing capability to the plant. We think this is a useful way of thinking about how tech suppliers should build new operating models. In our converged services model, we think that someday soon a single global service "manufacturing" capability would be able to produce multiple, discrete service products.

As we said in Chapter 3, many Level 2 suppliers have been struggling to articulate simply and clearly what their new model is and how they will transform their company as a result. For example, if you were a Level 2 enterprise software company readying your first SaaS offering, you would want to explain the "big picture" in a way that was easy for employees to understand. You might accomplish this with a simple internal white paper in which senior management:

- explains what a Level 3 operating model is and why it is right for SaaS.
- presents the targeted financial model for a Level 3 SaaS supplier.
- identifies which target market segments will be served using a Level 2 operating model and which will now be served via Level 3.
- draws out your Level 3 Tower of Power.
- lists the capabilities you need to fuel it. Identifies those that already exist and those that don't.
- articulates your plans to make or buy the missing ones and to update the existing ones when necessary.
- identifies where all those capabilities must "land" within the existing organizations. (Hopefully you are not creating lots of new ones!)
- states that employees will be trained to use the capabilities so they can begin to produce the new Level 3 SaaS offer successfully.
- provides a high-level project plan and a rough timeline for key milestones.

We realize there is a lot of executional complexity underneath these eight steps, but giving employees a simple primer on what you are trying to accomplish can work wonders.

The point is simply that by using the B4B framework and the notion of capabilities, we think that the new model transformation can be made evolutionary. That seems far more achievable than do the revolutionary changes we hear being discussed with much fear and trepidation by senior supplier executives who are expected to deliver both short-term profits and long-term growth. An orderly, capabilities-led transformation seems like just the thing they are looking for.

Then, if the CEO wants to go do an acquisition, you know what capabilities you are missing and whether a particular NewMo candidate can add to the production power of the core factory. Shortly, these new capabilities can be combined with existing ones to build a new supplier operating model that your Level 3 customers will love!

The Fish in the Middle

We just mentioned the dilemma facing executives whose shareholders want both short-term profits and long-term growth. This is a good description of the pressure facing roughly 100% of Level 2 suppler executives we talk with today. So let's discuss the financial dimension of a capabilities-led transformation.

This chapter has been focused on how to add new capabilities in a logical, orderly way. But because B4B is about *and*, not *or*, the cost of existing capabilities cannot be dropped, at least not right away. Until there are substantive reductions in product complexity (we really have to get to work on that!), high-tech and near-tech companies will still need lots of expensive sales and service people to conduct business.

As a result, any new capabilities that suppliers need to add in order to play at another supplier level are going to add to short-term costs. But that is not the worst of it. There is a second, often simultaneous problem, especially in moving to Level 3 or 4.

That second problem is a revenue problem, specifically the timing of those revenues. As we said at the end of Chapter 1, most Level 1 and 2 suppliers are used to getting paid up front. Once they deliver their technology, they are able to recognize the revenue and collect the cash. The only thing they must wait on is their extended maintenance contract revenue. But starting at Level 3, suppliers usually offer OpEx pricing models such as subscriptions or pay-for-consumption. So far, the evidence that many customers prefer that model is overwhelming. Many of the traditional software companies that made the brave move to OpEx pricing alternatives have been surprised by how many customers have switched. When they do, instead of getting a huge chunk of revenue up front, suppliers must wait and defer those revenues over an extended period of months or years. The contract amount may be the same, but the timing of the revenue recognition is not. If enough customers switch from the CapEx pricing model to the OpEx one, the supplier's short-term revenues dip compared to previous periods.

We drew these two transitions on a piece of paper using a status quo starting point. Then we drew one timeline that represents the short-term investment ramp-up period needed to create new organizational capabilities and a second timeline that represents the short-term revenue trough brought on by the shift to OpEx pricing models. Figure 6.5 shows what it looked like.

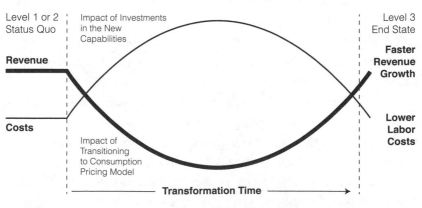

FIGURE 6.5 Journey to a Level 3 Operating Model

Yeah, OK, we know. It's a fish. Can't help that.

But know what? This fish must have been in a school at one time, because it turned out to be a pretty instructive creature.

On the far left, you see the status quo portrayed: fairly flat revenue with fairly stable costs. The space between those lines represents the profits of the supplier. The whole reason to embark on the journey is because of how those same two lines look on the far right (the "tail"). Revenues are now growing strongly thanks to the supplier's new Level 3 or 4 offers. At the same time, new technology-fueled and data-driven operating models are driving down its labor cost. The far right looks a lot more fun than the far left, don't you think?

The problem is the fish in the middle.

We don't know of anyone who has started at Level 1 or 2 and has successfully transformed its primary supplier operating model to Level 3 or 4 without experiencing the fish. It is the fish that has most Level 1 and 2 CEOs hesitating. At the same time, they frustratingly watch as many NewMo start-ups get to found their company starting at the far right. They get the benefits of the new model without having to worry about their time as a fish.

Although we can't completely eliminate the fish in the middle, what we have realized is that Level 1 and Level 2 suppliers can affect what type of fish they are going to be during the journey. The ones who plan poorly will be flounders: Their transformation will have a big fat body and a proportionately stubby tail. The ones who plan smartly using tactics such as those described earlier can be thought of as thresher sharks: Their transformation will have a skinny body with a very tall tail (see Figure 6.6). Threshers are fast and nimble.

If a supplier still has a healthy, growing core that does not require large revenue support from new model activities, then the portfolio strategy is fine. But for suppliers whose Level 2 core business is under pressure, we think the merge strategy has the best chance of making them a thresher and transforming the core, if they take a capabilities-led approach. They can pick up critical capabilities quickly via acquisition and pay for them by using the

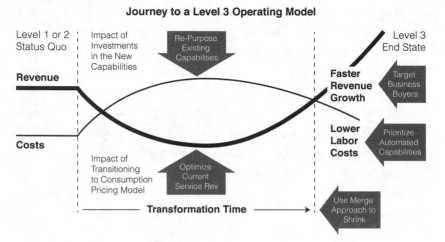

FIGURE 6.6 Journey to a Level 3 Operating Model

balance sheet rather than by using the income statement. Using some version of the eight-step approach we outlined, they can minimize the core's transformation time and increase the size and the angle of their tail.

Whether you are a Fortune 100 product company or a $10 million reseller, if you are in high-tech or near-tech, we think capabilities (not organizations) are the right way to think about transformation. If you think you have plenty of margin room, then maybe you can afford to create new organizations every time you have a new product, market, or operating model. We don't hear many of our 300 member companies describing themselves that way right now. Instead, they want to know how to be a thresher; they don't have much choice. Flounders are not an option for them. Just know that whether you develop your fish plan in-house or with outside help, we know of plenty of tactics to accelerate the journey and increase the height of your tail.

The Grand Bargain of Customer Capabilities

We have spent the first part of this chapter talking about how capabilities-led transformations work on the supplier side. But it also applies to how customers might think about the new supplier operating models they are starting to hear about. As we have said, things will be changing for both sides of the great divide. Just like the examples we cited in Chapter 2 of how consumer behavior needed to change in order for e-commerce to become what it is today, business customers must also be prepared to undergo some behavioral changes. Allowing suppliers access to data is but one aspect of the grand bargain that customers need to make with suppliers in B4B.

You see, there is the matter of who does what.

Suppliers are going to play new roles in order to provide Level 3 and Level 4 outcomes to customers. But if they are going to be playing more of a role, that means someone may be playing less of a role. Often, that someone is an employee at the customer's site. Thus begins the grand bargain.

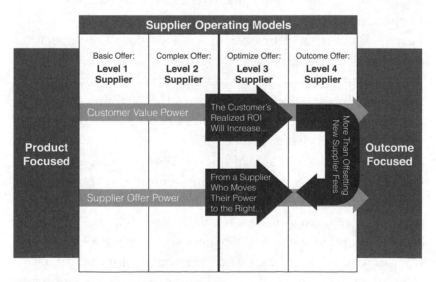

FIGURE 6.7 The Grand Bargain of B4B

The grand bargain, shown in Figure 6.7, is this: If a supplier takes a risk and makes these additional investments, and those

investments lead to capabilities that improve the financial outcomes the customer receives, then the customer must be willing
to return some of those benefits to the supplier in the form of
new revenue. If suppliers are not compensated for these new services, it will not be sustainable, and few will make the leap. That
would be a terrible loss for both sides. Thus, customers should
expect to see new fees accompanying the move in Supplier Offer
Power to the right. The fundamental economics of the B4B
proposition are compelling: Suppliers reduce the cost of technical complexity, and in their stead, new high-value services are offered. Although these services are costly, they yield much higher
overall returns to the customer. There should be new money to
spread around—that is, if customers are willing to change the
way they do business.

The first change, as we just mentioned, is who does what.
Most business customers have staffed up to operate and optimize
the technology they own. They have hired system administrators,
IT specialists, and production engineers—often lots of them. Now
Level 3 suppliers will be able to leverage their new operating
model to deliver many of the same roles at a far lower cost. But
these savings will only be realized if the business customers can
free themselves from some elements of their existing cost structure (see Figure 6.8). In order for one side to dial up its capabilities, the other side has to dial down.

Those are hard decisions to make. That may mean laying off
employees or reassigning them. It might mean that the size, budget, and influence of some in-house departments will shrink. It
may mean replacing current suppliers with whom you have a
good relationship with new suppliers who can move you to the
right along the Power Lines. These are hard decisions indeed. But
if customer departments such as IT, production, or operations are
to be fiscally responsible and deliver on the demand to increase
the ROI from the company's technology spend, these are decisions that must be made.

**Suppliers Play Roles Once Seen as the
Job of Internal Staff (IT, Ops, etc.)**

FIGURE 6.8 Suppliers Play Roles Once Seen as the Job of Internal Staff

Another thing that will surely change is the supplier selection process itself. The old RFP criteria that customers used when selecting Level 1 and Level 2 suppliers are going to need a major overhaul. Throughout this book, we have discussed myriad new capabilities and roles that suppliers will offer. Most business customers will need to think quite differently about what the important attributes of a winning near-tech or high-tech supplier will look like. In addition, suppliers must start the new practice of qualifying customers. In an era of shared risk and consumption-based pricing, they need to ensure that a potential customer is actually capable of attaining the target volume outcome before they invest their resources and capabilities. This will be a whole new experience for customers, one they may not like at first. However, such a process could be massively productive in uncovering weaknesses and landmines that historically would not have been discovered until a project was on the brink of failure.

We also think customers will adopt new tactics on their journey to expensive global technology solutions. Rather than looking for a sole-source, enterprise-wide supplier at the outset, they may be inclined to try one or more pilot projects with one or more different suppliers. This notion of "land and expand" will become far more practical in the Level 3 XaaS world than it ever was in the world of on-premise, CapEx Level 2 operating models. We think this will become so common as to have a big impact on how suppliers and customers develop their partnerships.

These are just a few of the many customer implications of the ascendency of Level 3 and Level 4 suppliers over the next few years. The new bridges spanning the great divide could significantly change how suppliers and customers select and engage with each other. We are on the verge of something powerful. The changes will be worth it. But what are the first moves, and who makes them?

The Three Pivots

Earlier in the book, we talked about how the onus was on suppliers to make the first moves on the topic of data security. That is only fair. After all, they are the suppliers, not the customers. They have to earn the business, to demonstrate that they have the Tower of Power necessary to play seriously at Level 3 or 4. But we think there are three things that both suppliers and customers can start working on immediately.

Why do we call them the Three Pivots? Well, a pivot requires that something stays in place while something else moves. In a spreadsheet, a pivot table has a fixed body of data, but there are different ways to sort or add it. In the sport of basketball, when a player is not dribbling the ball, one foot must stay in place, but the other foot is free to move to a new position. This is the idea that we think both customers and suppliers must keep in mind as they begin their transformations to Level 3 and Level 4 partnerships. They can't just run away from everything that exists today and start all over. Instead, they need to keep some things still while other things move. That is exactly what high-tech and near-tech markets need to be doing right now in order to begin their transformations.

The Three Pivots are:

- land-and-expand selling.
- adoption services.
- the data handshake.

While there are hundreds of transformational activities that suppliers and their customers could act on, the Three Pivots are probably the most important. They are activities that most NewMo suppliers have already begun working on. They are activities that, if not begun, threaten to make Level 2 suppliers look out of date. Finally, they are activities that absolutely will not succeed without the support and engagement of customers.

So, let's get to work.

7 | Pivot 1: Land + Expand Selling

THE FIRST PIVOT REQUIRED TO WIN IN B4B IS TO RETHINK HOW customer-supplier partnerships will be developed. The core sales motions within established suppliers have a lot of inertia to them. Suppliers adjust their pricing continuously, reinvent their marketing every few quarters, and reengineer their product lines every few years. However, the core sales model in those same companies today would still look very familiar to Mr. Patterson.

If customers were not changing their expectations much or quickly, this would not be a problem. Suppliers and customers could just continue with the sales and purchasing processes that have gotten them to where they are. The challenge is that consumption-based business models are crossing the chasm, and the new customer expectations that come along with them are beginning to represent a material part of many suppliers' sales pipelines.

Beginning at Level 3, B4B is likely to drive a fundamental redesign of sales methodologies, roles, coverage models, organization structures, and compensation plans. In this chapter, we lay out a playbook for what the sales force of the future may look like as these changes take hold. Specifically, we propose a new mandate and a more modern set of partnering motions for Level 3 and

Level 4 suppliers and their customers to consider. It will be up to suppliers to determine how aggressively they shift their go-to-market strategy toward this new model, and if they must execute both the old and the new sales playbooks in parallel for a time. It will be up to customers to decide if that supplier is moving fast enough.

Selling Has Proved Difficult to Innovate

Before we jump to the prescription, let's spend a few minutes on what sales looks like in nearly every high-tech and near-tech company we know. It's not that sales is broken, per se; it's just proven to be hard to innovate.

For most sales organizations, the last major innovation was called solution selling. The term itself is attributed to a sales manager at Wang Laboratories in the 1970s.[1] Through its various iterations, solution selling taught sales teams to group their offerings as packaged solutions instead of individual point products. Sales reps were told to ask customers what keeps them up at night, and then find something in what the customer said that linked back to one of the prepackaged solutions in their bag.

Did this work? Absolutely. It was definitely an improvement over what might be called "product selling." That went something like this: "Let me show you all the amazing features, speeds, and feeds that my product has, and I am sure you need at least one of them." Solution selling started with the customer's challenges, not the product's features. That was a definite improvement.

However, we argue that its effectiveness began to decline about a decade ago. Customers had heard the word "solutions" used ad nauseam. They often began to feel like the supplier's sales rep was pushing something again. This time, it was a package rather than a product. To further complicate matters, it became clear that many of the "solutions" were less integrated in practice than in Power-Point. They were more like preset order bundles than faster ways to achieve business value.

Some symptoms of a solution selling model slowly running out of gas are worth highlighting. Over the last decade, we have witnessed four troubling trends in high-tech and near-tech sales organizations:

1. **Drive-By Selling:** The cardinal rule of solution selling is to qualify up front whether the customer has budget for the solution the sales rep is selling. The unintended consequence has been that sales reps actually spend less time on what might classically be considered "selling." If customers do not have budget ready to commit, they are encouraged to find a customer that does. We call this "drive-by selling." At a time when our products are more complicated than ever, some suppliers are actually teaching their sales teams not to spend time helping customers understand the offer's advanced value so that the customer can create new budget to invest in them.

2. **Overlays on Overlays:** At the same time that some customers have become immune to solution selling, complexity has raced to the stars. In response, high-tech and near-tech sales leaders have added specialized sales overlays to try to close the gap. For some suppliers, these overlay teams are in the form of vertical industry experts. For others, they are product specialists focused on sets of technologies or "architectures." These suppliers have ended up with 16-legged sales calls: an account manager, a sales engineer, an industry expert, a technical solutions expert from each of the three major technologies a customer cares about, a services sales rep, and a business development manager from the internal consulting organization. When the sales team members outnumber the customer in a sales meeting by two to one, you know you have a problem. These overlays are the best response suppliers have been able to come up with so far. But they are neither meeting most suppliers' substantial growth expectations nor remediating their declining sales productivity.

3. **Increasing Channel Concentration:** To help resolve this complexity, many customers are now placing their trust in systems integrators or cloud service providers. From the customer's perspective, this gives them "one throat to choke," that is, a small number of trusted advisors that can work across multiple product companies or across the individual business units within product companies. Product companies, in turn, are seeing a dramatic increase in channel concentration where fewer and fewer go-to-market partners represent more and more of their business. The impact of this is profound. Near-term, it forces product companies to succumb to aggressive reseller discount pressure as these channel partners leverage their scale. Longer-term, it can even lead to channel partners "designing out" premium products in favor of third-party offerings or even their own technology. Some very large customers are taking a similar approach. Google's engineering of its own networking gear and column-based database are good examples.

4. **Rising Cost of Sales:** For all of the reasons we mentioned in Chapter 3, many shareholders are starting to question the continued viability of high-growth promises by high-tech and near-tech suppliers. Those above-market growth rates have historically been the basis for above-market valuations. However, these growth rates are now in the low single digits (or worse) for many of the industry leaders. Without this growth, the suppliers' overlay sales teams have swollen the cost of sales and have driven increasingly higher expense-to-booking (E:B) ratios. This is what keeps the suppliers' heads of sales, CFOs, and CEOs most on edge. Their sales teams have been running as hard as they can up a down escalator for some time. E:B ratios seem to be getting higher, not lower, and the trend seems to be accelerating.

We think the advent of Level 3 and Level 4 operating models are a good time for a ground-up rethinking of the sales model. Trying harder, tweaking compensation, augmenting coverage, adding overlays, and bundling products just will not get us where we need to go in B4B.

The New Sales Discussions

We have tried to put into Figure 7.1 a synthesis of what high-tech and near-tech suppliers are hearing their customers say. This is not easy, of course, because customers and suppliers are often using different words to describe what is fundamentally the same thing.

Imagine a speedometer for the sales discussions between the two parties. One needle shows the chronology of sales discussions on the traditional offer of high-tech and near-tech Level 1 or 2 offers. The other shows the evolution of customer interests in the consumption-based models of B4B. Each needle sweeps in a progression from the earliest customer discussion at the bottom to the last stage discussion at the top.

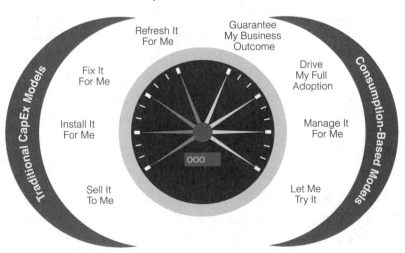

The New Spectrum of Sales Discussions

FIGURE 7.1 The New Spectrum of Sales Discussions

The left side of Figure 7.1 is familiar to most high-tech and near-tech suppliers. Some customers are happy just to have the supplier sell them a product with a view that their internal staff or a third party will make that product valuable to them (Level 1). Others want their supplier to do more, such as "Install it for me," "Fix it for me," or even "Refresh it for me" (Level 2). However, if customers just wanted the left side of the speedometer, we would not be writing this book.

On the right side, some customers are just now beginning to try cloud and consumption-based models while others are already done with that stage. The latter may be shifting whole parts of their high-tech and near-tech installed base to the consumption-based models of B4B. In IT, that means their massive server farms, storage area networks, enterprise applications, and mission-critical equipment are all up for grabs. Capital budgets are being cut, and "pay as you grow" is the new mantra. In hospitals, this may mean that suppliers will own, manage, or even operate entire layers of equipment such as smart beds or CT scanners. Manufacturing customers may want to purchase all-in bundles in which they pay a precision measurement component supplier just a few cents for every unit of production-line output that meets a certain quality standard.

As Figure 7.1 illustrates, customers who are considering these models can generally be segmented into four levels of expectations in terms of what they want their supplier partners to do for them. The simplest is "Let me try it." As we will discuss below, there is a spirit of "fit for purpose" and experimentation that is essential for customers who are new to Level 3 and Level 4 offers. Next are customers who say, "Manage it for me," or "Drive my full adoption" (Level 3). A few customers have already moved to Level 4 of B4B. They are contracting directly for the business outcome they seek to achieve.

So here is the rub: Some supplier sales motions are stuck in an approach invented for the left side of Figure 7.1 when many of their largest customers have moved over to the right side. Customer expectations and the sales discussions that link to them have changed more in the last five years than in any previous five-year period. It is time for a new plan.

The New Sales Mandate

So if a supplier and a customer could get together, take out a clean sheet of paper, and describe how a supplier's sales organization could best benefit both sides in the new world, could they agree on something? If so, what would they write? What would that new sales mandate be? In 40 words or less, here is a starting point from which they could work:

> *Sales will help customers capture the maximum amount of value from an advanced technology in the minimum amount of time. By doing so, Sales will accelerate the growth of our partnership over every one-quarter, one-year, and three-year time horizon.*

This mandate differs from the current practice for most suppliers we know in four key ways. First, it forces sales teams to get on the customer's side of the table by truly understanding the value they seek to achieve. It is no longer good enough to stop listening when the business problem is clear enough to pull a "solution" out of your bag.

Second, this mandate requires sales reps to become experts in the business value generated by the advanced capabilities of their offers. When we say "advanced capabilities," we don't mean just the faster speeds and feeds. We mean the capabilities that can return 10 times the potential investment for customers. Those advanced capabilities are what venture capitalists focus their companies' sales teams on; suppliers and customers should too.

Third, this new sales mandate balances the three horizons of growth that shareholders on both sides care about most. Too many sales teams today are winning the battle (making the quarter) but are losing the war (underperforming against longer-term growth expectations). In valuation terms, these sales teams deliver the "E," near-term earnings, but not the "P/E," the price/earnings multiple that speaks to how confident shareholders are in the company's long-term prospects for profitable growth.

Just delivering on these three new sales mandates is going to require fundamental changes in suppliers' core sales motions. In many cases, suppliers may need more than one sales model (as shown in Figure 7.2). Make the transition early and powerfully enough, and suppliers will accelerate their growth, especially at Level 3. Stick to the current approach too long, and you will be faced with an untenable cost of sales when customers shift their buying behavior to consumption-based models.

B4B: Different Sales Models Evolve

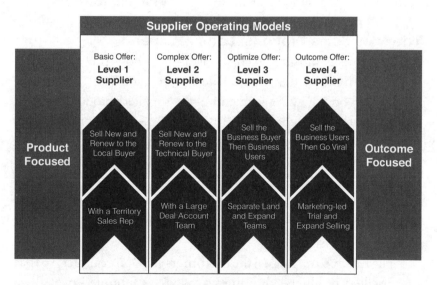

FIGURE 7.2 B4B: Different Sales Models Evolve

Finally, the new mandate positions the sales organization for a world of consumption-based business models. Customers are "voting with their feet" at an ever-increasing rate. When they do not realize the value they seek in the time frame they expected, they simply stop paying for the offer and adopt someone else's. One of the authors experienced this firsthand, writing off a brand-new $20 million CRM system from a leading enterprise software company within 90 days of going live. In this case, the frontline sellers revolted over the complexity of the system that the first supplier created. It was forcing them to spend two-plus hours per day on data entry instead of on selling. The big winner was salesforce.com, which, with full frontline and senior executive support, had a replacement system up and running in 90 days for a multibillion-dollar company. Such an extreme example might have been rare in 2005 when it happened. Today, it is anything but.

This new sales mandate is right for the times ahead. To see how these new practices might differ, let's contrast some of the traditional selling motions of Levels 1 and 2 with the new models being developed by leading Level 3 and 4 suppliers.

The New Sales Motions: Land + Expand

Most high-tech and near-tech suppliers we know run a common set of sales motions that we call New + Renew. The "New" sales motion sold both new deployments of the supplier's products and the service contracts attached to them. The "Renew" sales motion administered and renewed those service contracts for as long as possible.

This made a lot of sense at Levels 1 and 2. The new team did the heavy lifting: selling the customer on the product, generating substantial up-front cash flow, and growing the installed base. Their compensation was front-loaded to reflect the value they secured for the supplier.

The renew team helped the customers stay "on contract" so that the installed products continued to work as intended over their life cycle. They also occasionally sold some incremental project-based services around the product. However, their main focus and most of their compensation were ultimately tied to making sure annual service contract renewal rates stayed high and service margins stayed strong.

The new sales team was where the tough selling action was, and the renew sales organization focused more on installed base and contract management. Inside many suppliers, the new team was considered to be the senior team and the renew team was seen as the junior team. As shown in Figure 7.3, this might have made sense when your business model was highly dependent on product sales and product-attached services.

Legacy Sales Motions: New + Renew

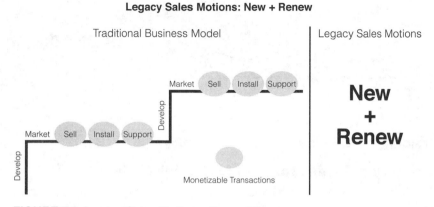

FIGURE 7.3 Legacy Sales Motions: New + Renew

Consumption-based business models have flipped this on its head. In an "as-a-service" world, the initial deal is really an option on future revenue and profit. The big, profitable financial outcome for the supplier is by no means guaranteed as it was in the old world. The lifetime value of a customer is now predicated on their full, widespread adoption of the advanced capabilities of the offer and the rapid achievement of their business value goals.

Few sales organizations are ready for this fundamental transformation in how customers are evaluating, acquiring, deploying, adopting, managing, and evolving their solutions. As shown in Figure 7.4, this future business model demands that high-tech and near-tech suppliers add two new sales motions: Land + Expand.

So let's spend some time on what these Land + Expand sales motions will look like and how they are different from the model suppliers have been running for so long.

Future Sales Motions: Land + Expand

Consumption Business Model   Future Sales Motions

Support
& Sell
Offer
& Sell
Support
& Sell
Offer
& Sell

Market   Sell   Install

Develop

Monetizable Transactions

**Land
+
Expand**

FIGURE 7.4 Future Sales Motions: Land + Expand

Key Capabilities for the Land Sales Motion

Over the last 18 months, we have been working with many high-tech and near-tech early adopters of Land + Expand selling. Some were pure SaaS companies, whereas others were making a transition to consumption-based models. Once these suppliers started with consumption-based business models (or acquired companies that did), they found that they had to run a "land" sales motion that looks a lot like Figure 7.5.

Future Sales Motions: Land

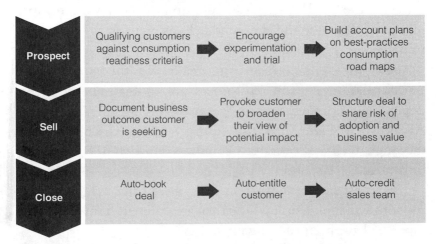

Prospect	Qualifying customers against consumption readiness criteria	→	Encourage experimentation and trial	→	Build account plans on best-practices consumption road maps
Sell	Document business outcome customer is seeking	→	Provoke customer to broaden their view of potential impact	→	Structure deal to share risk of adoption and business value
Close	Auto-book deal	→	Auto-entitle customer	→	Auto-credit sales team

FIGURE 7.5 Future Sales Motions: Land

A few new sales capabilities and activities are called for in land selling.

As we mentioned in Chapter 6, many customers may like the idea of consumption-based pricing models but might not want to make minimum commitments. Because consumption-based pricing shares and aligns risk, suppliers then earn the right to ask up front about the customer's adoption preparedness. For the supplier, expending the resources to pursue customers that think they want a Level 3 partnership, but can't or won't successfully consume it, is a bad decision. That customer adds cost to the supplier's sales and services motions without adding any incremental revenue. In those cases, exiting from the sales cycle early is actually better than winning the deal. This is going to take a lot of maturity for both suppliers and customers to accept. But it is necessary.

Second, customers who are excited about the new business models often do not know exactly what to ask for. As part of the land sales motion, suppliers need to create options for customers to explore the potential of their solutions at a minimal cost. This is a proven play in the B2C e-commerce world. An increasing number of Level 3 SaaS suppliers such as salesforce.com have been making available free trial options of their offers. Level 4 suppliers such as Amazon are using a similar approach. They have innovated enterprise infrastructure through per-minute billing options and automated tools that suggest to customers the specific price plan that would drive their lowest cost based on their actual usage. Can you imagine if your cell phone company did that? You would never be on the wrong pricing package again. This is the new face of what, in the old world of selling, would have been called "lead generation." This is using a marketing-led approach to get customers to experience their service platform, knowing that it will ultimately sell products.

Third, consumption-based models bring down the cost, complexity, and risk of high-tech and near-tech solutions. For those who remember their Economics 101 class, when cost/complexity/risk fall significantly, demand generally goes up dramatically. Economists call this the shape of the demand curve as customers who were put off by previous offers flood the market. You will call this sales velocity. In land selling, sales professionals need to be constantly aware of this increase in addressable market. They need to provoke customers to think differently about the pace at which their offers can add value and, therefore, the pace at which customers should be consuming them. In the land sales motion, we call these best-practice consumption road maps. The Land + Expand selling model often helps reduce presales costs to the supplier because not everything has to be worked out up front. The customer is not risking overspending or underspending. They can start with the basics and grow into a complex solution over time. That should help reduce the need for all the overlay sales capabilities that are required to ensure a complete enterprise solution design before the customer can comfortably commit.

Finally, in B4B, the new sales organization's new best friend is named "auto," as in auto-quote, auto-configure, auto-close, auto-book, auto-provision, auto-entitle, and auto-sales credit. When a new deal is just an option on future revenue but not a guarantee of it, you really cannot afford a lot of friction in sales operations. Sales needs to be frictionless and scalable. Too many suppliers making the pivot to B4B are still using their legacy IT systems that require multiple people to manually touch most of the deals. This reduces profitability in the near-term and inhibits suppliers' ability to scale over the long term.

So the capabilities and activities required in the "land" sales motion of B4B are often different from those of the "new" sales motion that most suppliers are familiar with. Often, these differences may even affect how the supplier organizes its sales function.

Organizing for Land Selling

Land selling demands an organization that can overcome an ever-increasing range of competitive offers to make a supplier the leader in the markets in which it competes—one that constructively resets the buying criteria customers are using as they migrate their purchases of high-tech and near-tech to Level 3 and beyond. It is also one that helps each customer capture the maximum amount of business value in the minimum period.

Emerging Level 3 leaders are generally setting up two separate sales teams: a land team that owns selling new customers or securing commitments for major new deployments from existing customers, and an expand team that maximizes the lifetime value delivered to customers and their increasing consumption of offers. This runs contrary to how most high-tech and near-tech companies are structured today. Most have a product sales team and a services sales team. In a B4B world, the line between what is a product and what is a service is so blurry that it may no longer be the right concept around which to organize.

Salesforce.com has used this approach to outgrow both tech industry incumbents and attackers alike, redefining a big swath of the software industry in the process. Specifically, Land + Expand enabled salesforce.com to broaden its reach from the SMB customers of its early days to include huge deployments in large, global enterprises. At salesforce.com, the land sales team grows the customer base, whereas the expand team, what it calls the "Customers for Life" team, accelerates customer adoption, business value, and advanced feature consumption. The same organization also renews and expands customer contracts.

In this model, the land team owns selling in three deal categories: first-time purchases to new "logos," the significant expansion of existing purchases to new regions or divisions that have not previously adopted them, and major cross-sells of adjacent offers (e.g., service cloud sold into a sales cloud customer at salesforce.com). Either way, the land sellers are securing for the supplier options on long-term revenues.

Many sales professionals from traditional B2B selling models are successfully transitioned into these land selling roles. The good ones know that B4B has been coming for several years.

Companies are finding that their best sellers, once trained in the land sales motion, are able to ramp up quickly.

B4B favors sellers that have consistently invested in building new skills, relationships, and competencies over time. They speak the language of the customers through vertical industry knowledge and business acumen. They have relationships both in the technical departments of customers and in the lines of business. These key relationships allow them to land new deals as decision-making power shifts. They understand and practice provocation-based selling[2] to create new budgets for customers, not just solution selling to consume budgets that already exist.

So we've covered how to organize a land team and with whom to staff that team. We've left the biggest issue for last: how to compensate those land sellers. Now let's agree up front that legacy sales compensation just does not work very well in consumption- or outcome-based pricing models. A specific example might help demonstrate why.

We recently came across a single sales region within a major tech supplier that had more than 10 consumption-based deals in its pipeline, each of which was shown as having a value of more than $25 million. That's the good news. The customers were excited about this supplier's newly introduced and recently acquired cloud-based offers and were ready to move ahead with major deployments. In fact, they were mostly swapping out legacy deployments and shifting to consumption-based models for the replacement solutions. The customers really felt that in moving to a diversified portfolio approach including both traditional and consumption-based offers, the supplier in question had "heard their feedback." Customer interest was so high that there were "Way to go!" voice mails from senior execs for all involved.

Here was the problem: Although these deals had the *potential* for $25 million, the customers did not want to be legally bound to the full number of users from Day 1 of these deployments. In fact, some of them might actually start with only a small number for the first quarter or two. These customers liked the pay-as-you-grow approach that they had experienced with other Level 3 suppliers. In fact, one of the CIOs in question even explained to the supplier's regional executive that, in this new world, his internal IT organization had to "earn in" with their lines of business over time. There was no way he could sign a binding up-front commitment even if he wanted to. His internal customers were free to adopt at the speed that made sense for their respective businesses.

So how do suppliers successfully compensate these land sales professionals when that type of customer commitment is the new reality? Well, matching sales professionals' incentive compensation to the timing of revenue seems to make sense, until a supplier actually tries to do it. At that moment, their best salespeople walk out the door to a competitor still executing on the CapEx model. Yet, relaxing their booking criteria to include "pro forma" or "planned" consumption over the typical three to five years of these deals does not make sense either. That would fail to incorporate the substantial risks of full adoption of advanced capabilities and fast time-to-business value that stand between the pro forma deal size and the actual one.

What most companies are experimenting with is a hybrid between the two. That is, giving their land sales professionals a partial incentive on the overall breadth of the customer relationship in parallel with more traditional incentive compensation on committed bookings. This aligns compensation with what you really want them to do: setting up customers for full consumption of your solutions over time while also locking in some up-front commitments. Maybe that ratio could be 50:50.

Key Capabilities for the Expand Sales Motion

Once a supplier has landed a new customer or a major new deployment of their platform within an existing customer, the real work begins. Again, new capabilities are needed. This is the period of true value capture for both sides—the supplier and the customer. The supplier needs to exercise all those options on revenue that the land sales motion has delivered. As you will see in the following discussion, one of the biggest changes in B4B is that simply renewing a customer or just keeping them "satisfied" is just not good enough anymore. Both are table stakes. If the expand sales motion is executed well, then renewals either go away entirely or become non-events. Let's dig into how the expand sales motion, shown in Figure 7.6, connects customer value to supplier revenue.

Future Sales Motions: Expand

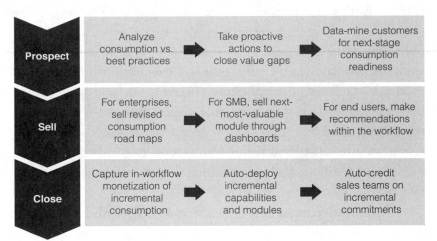

FIGURE 7.6 Future Sales Motions: Expand

Few Level 2 suppliers have a sales motion in their company today that looks like the one shown in Figure 7.6. They may have some activities underway in separate groups that reflect parts of it. However, we have not seen a single company, at any level, pull all of this together at scale yet. There are three major areas to focus on: adoption services, expand coverage models, and in-the-workflow commerce.

First, the expand sales motion is predicated on customers' full adoption of the advanced capabilities of supplier offers and the rapid capture of the full business value customers were seeking when they first deployed their solution. Without those two achievements, there is no ongoing customer relationship under B4B, let alone expansions of it. So the expand sales motion actually starts on Day 2 of the customer life cycle with your company. This is also where the critical role played by the adoption services organization pays off.

To enable this "Day 2 mind-set," product companies must have the capability and the data to fully instrument their solutions (a topic we cover in detail in Pivot 3: The Data Handshake) so that they can assess where every customer is relative to best-practice adoption and value capture. They will use these insights to take action with customers early on in order to close any gaps utilizing all the service activities we'll define in Pivot 2: Adoption Services. These actions might be as simple as incremental online training for a given set of users or a corrective action plan discussion at the next quarterly business review. They could be as sophisticated as using every inbound customer support call to position one incremental advanced feature that a specific user is not yet using. There is much experimentation going on, but it all resolves down to this: Level 3 and Level 4 leaders are putting themselves fully in service to the achievement of their customers' desired business outcomes.

Second, suppliers are rethinking their coverage models under B4B. As we wrote in *Consumption Economics*, the balance of power for high-tech and near-tech decision making is swinging from central command and control to decentralized business departments and users.[3] As a result, suppliers are rapidly learning they must love the little dots of upsell and cross-sell revenue much more than they used to. In the expand sales motion, this means that the number of customer employees or the total customer revenue is no longer a sufficient way to segment your sales team. To maximize the lifetime revenue of a customer, suppliers now need to sell both high and broad—large transactions and little ones.

Even large corporations are going to look and feel like many smaller companies in terms of how they make high-tech and near-tech purchase decisions. So although their land sales teams are covering the major corporate buying centers, suppliers need expand sales teams covering all those departments and users that will ultimately be making more and more purchase decisions on their own. In health care, this could be individual hospitals in a hospital group or in individual departments within a hospital. In manufacturing, this could be each of the major factories and the functional groups within them.

So when you see the terms "enterprise," "SMB," and "end users" in the preceding sales motion, similar expand motions could now be needed all within a single large customer corporation. Enterprise could be the corporate buying center in which the expand sales motion does high-touch selling of large extensions to the consumption road map that your land team first positioned with the customer. SMB could mean the presentation of specific next-most-valuable modules to a specific department. End-user selling could mean helping customers to fully consume both the advanced capabilities they have already paid for and the next-in-line ones they have not yet purchased. This is expand sales coverage in B4B.

An essential part of expand selling is the enablement of in-the-workflow commerce capability. Few enterprise high-tech and near-tech suppliers are able to meet these expectations today. It requires the modularization of both their offers and the pricing plans associated with them. It requires new management tools that help companies define which sets of modules should be available to which end-user communities. It requires expand selling algorithms that make intelligent, user-specific suggestions within the workflow. Finally, it requires a commerce engine that can either "bill back" to a central funding source pre-negotiated with the customer or charge an end user's credit card directly. Almost every Level 3 or Level 4 supplier we know is leaving money on the table by not yet enabling users to get the exact set of features they need given their specific role, working style, and level of sophistication. Once again, a capabilities-led approach to transformation makes sense.

Finally, customers must also be willing to change their command-and-control thinking as it relates to technology spending. The era of one-size-fits-all-users is over. The new generation of consumer devices has created a completely different set of expectations for how much end users should be able to tailor the tools that allow them to do their jobs. This is true in every industry and nearly every country. No two iPhones are alike within a couple weeks after leaving their shiny white box. They don't just look different. They function differently too because consumers pick the apps they want to use. This App Store mind-set is coming to the business world. What it means for the expand sales motion is that end users and the departments in which they work will need substantial latitude in order to efficiently grow their consumption of value.

So customer executives must find innovative but controllable approaches to enable this new path to full end-user productivity. They simply can't require an employee end user to march a purchase order through the purchasing department every time he or she wants to add a new feature set. They need to develop a more modern approach that allows the little dots of consumption to be auto-approved and auto-controlled. This is a part of Pivot 3: The Data Handshake.

Organizing for Expand Selling

Before talking about organization, per se, suppliers need to list the capabilities that their expand sales team needs to have. This is the same approach we suggested in Chapter 6. By doing this, they can identify where in their current organization these capabilities likely exist today—the "what" before the "who," if you will. To execute the expand sales motion, suppliers are going to need four main capabilities: annuity selling skills, low-cost customer interactions, sophisticated propensity to buy models, and modular offer management.

The need for annuity selling skills is obvious. In our experience, many sales professionals who have grown up in product sales roles do not prefer to play the expand role. They have grown up with an idea of "lead gen" driving demand. The idea of working tirelessly to create incremental demand within existing customers via best-practice consumption models runs against what many in product sales know how to do, and maybe even like to do. Plus, their high compensation expectations may make such a role economically unfeasible for them. A low cost-per-customer touch is critical given that many expand offers are going to be those little dots or "micro transactions" we talked about earlier. Suppliers simply cannot afford to run the expand sales motion effectively without a huge number of customer touches at a low cost per touch. Levels 3 and 4 call for the enablement of "volume operations selling," not "complex systems selling." It means that suppliers could soon generate a billion dollars in revenue through a million incremental bumps in consumption, not just through another 50 big deals.

Insightful, big data and analytics-driven "propensity-to-buy models" are needed to ensure that the expand sales motion never feels as though "we have this next module on sale for a limited time." Suppliers need the capability to be on the customers' side of the table with a fact-based understanding of their current usage and adoption and the uncanny (data and analytics on top of Success Science) ability to know what customers need next (even before they do).

Finally, modular offer management capabilities are going to be important in reconstituting a supplier's monolithic solutions into the bite-sized chunks of capability that customers can buy in the expand sales motion. No product manager has ever been given that challenge. Most are still stuck in "good/better/best" bundles.

So suppliers will need at least these four major capabilities to be successful in executing this new expand sales motion at scale.

Let's now turn our attention to where they might have those capabilities today. The biggest concentration of annuity selling skills today is likely within a supplier's services sales force. However, this organization will not be a perfect fit. Too many sellers in service sales have "made their number" over the years simply working on (single-dimension) maintenance contract renewals. They certainly have not had the same (multi-dimension) focus on expand selling that we are talking about here. They have been satisfied with continuous improvement in the renewal rates on offers initially sold by others. So if this group is going to be the seed for a supplier's new expand sales team, there is going to be some substantial rework required in incentives, training, metrics, and skills.

As we discussed in the last chapter, beyond purely electronic interactions, the lowest cost-per-customer touch in a supplier today is likely in your customer support organization. In fact, inbound calls from customers are among the greatest underleveraged opportunities for the expand sales motion that are immediately available to them. Interestingly, salesforce.com figured this out very early by structuring the Customers for Life team to include both expand selling and customer support. This positions them to use every inbound customer interaction to not just get the customer's case resolved, but to also drive their adoption of advance capabilities and incremental consumption. This is the purest form of B4B, but one with lots of potential upside still to be realized. The hand-offs are not perfected. There is still a lot of work to be done to effectively and productively link adoption services with expand selling. Suppliers will need to make some changes in how support engineers are trained, how they are measured, what consumption analytics they monitor, what actions they take, and how they share leads with expand selling teams. There is a fine line between supporting and commercializing a trusted advisor relationship, one that cannot be crossed without great damage to the partnership. The guiding principle we provided in *Consumption Economics* was this: Helping will sell, but selling won't help.[4]

Propensity-to-buy models are a new capability for most tech suppliers. They might have done some analysis of what the characteristics of their best prospects are versus their worst ones. However, they have likely never made the investment in the data scientists needed to run a powerful B4B expand sales force. We'll cover this in more detail in the next chapter.

Finally, modular offer management skills might exist in two places inside supplier organizations today. If they have a group called services product management, services product marketing, or services portfolio management, they might have already started down this path toward deep modularization of their offers. That is, taking products and wrapping them in consumption-based service offers that are more readily consumable. The other place where they may have existing capabilities is in their field marketing teams who are often tasked with developing offers for market or regional segmentation. Either way, these groups have likely been thinking incrementally within the context of a supplier's existing offers and business model. Now they need to go further. They need to ask the question, "What would Apple do?" as they develop the path from the "one-size-perfectly-fits-few" offers of today to the highly modular ones of tomorrow.

So while most suppliers are not starting from scratch in building an organization that can execute expand selling at scale, our bet is that there is a lot of organizational resistance to bringing all of this together. As we just said, we hear over and over again the debate about the "separation of church and state" issue of blending customer support with expand selling: "Won't that decrease our customer satisfaction?" "Won't customers be frustrated with us for selling them when they don't want to be sold to?" "Our compensation systems and metrics just won't allow us to mix these teams." The reality is that, done right, the expand sales motion will drive higher customer satisfaction, broader adoption, and faster business value capture. Here is the bottom line in our view: This approach actually reduces customer risk. They get just what they need, just when they need it. And we are not talking about doing that according to some high-level technology architecture road map, but at the actual business user level where it really makes a difference.

Put simply, this is a far better way for customers to purchase and consume technology. Customers should thank suppliers for going with them to B4B instead of staying with the current high-risk, high-complexity approach.

The other area of resistance is the question of where all this new capability should report to inside the supplier. There are really three options.

Option A for suppliers is to continue having the land sales team report to the overall head of sales and the expand selling team report to the head of services. This is the least disruptive to the status quo and may be the best answer if they expect to have at least three to five years during which consumption-based models represent only a small portion of overall revenues. That means they assume that Level 1 or 2 CapEx models will continue to be where the buying action is going to remain for an extended time. It could also be the right answer if other major changes are going on in their product sales organization. Finally, the services organization may also be a safe place to incubate and debug the Land + Expand sales motion until the company and customers are ready for it. But this option requires a head of services that is up to the task both in terms of their buy-in to the "helping can sell" mentality as well as their sales management skill set. If that executive is in place today, Option A is a great answer.

Option B entails moving away from the organizational separation of product and services sales by putting all sales under one leader and reconstituting the frontline selling resources into future-state Land + Expand teams. We think the power of this model is that suppliers will find that the faster they get to the true expand sales motion, the more they can accelerate both their legacy and consumption-based business revenues. That's because driving full adoption of advanced features and rapid time-to-business value will accelerate refresh cycles on the old model, not just incremental consumption on the new one. The biggest danger in this model is that it separates adoption and support services from expand selling—services loses its responsibility for driving revenue and profit, becoming just another cost center for suppliers' CFOs to micro-manage. Remember, beginning at Level 3, the supplier's whole offer starts to become one great big service platform. The last thing you want to do is to cost-manage that customer experience into nothingness. Very strong and clear accounting linkages need to be made between the investment in services and the revenue generated by the separate expand sales organization. The supplier cannot conclude that adoption services and expand selling are two separate thoughts.

Option C is a middle ground that works best for suppliers structured around two or three major divisions in which the supplier levels differ. Basically, they maintain the New + Renew sales motions within the sales force for their Level 1 or 2 CapEx business units while building the new Option A or B Land + Expand sales motions for their Level 3 or Level 4 as-a-service division(s). This model works best when as-a-service businesses compete in different markets than the CapEx businesses do (at least over the next three to five years) and sell in different buying centers. Citrix is a good example here. It's enjoyed exceptional growth running a version of Land + Expand in their SaaS/Go-To-Meeting division in parallel with a more traditional model in its IT infrastructure businesses. It is sometimes easier to incubate a new model for a part of the business than trying to move the whole company to B4B selling all at once.

Bringing It All Together

The sales pivot of B4B may very well be the hardest one for suppliers and customers to stomach. Land + Expand selling requires the development of a clean-sheet model for the activities of the supplier sales professionals and the people who support them. It repurposes product sales, service sales, and customer support teams in a significantly different way for a very different outcome, that is, maximizing customer adoption of your advanced capabilities en route to more business value for customers and more revenue for suppliers. For customers, this means empowering business buyers and end users to make more technology decisions. It means updating heavy, old purchasing processes to handle little dot transactions. It also means that they must get comfortable with suppliers engaged more actively in expanding the partnership.

Put simply, Land + Expand is a different approach for a different mandate, as shown in Figure 7.7.

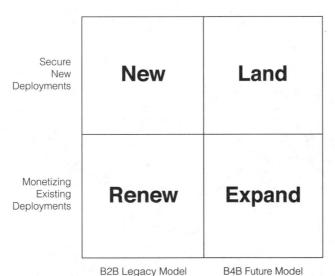

FIGURE 7.7 The Future of Sales

Most high-tech and near-tech suppliers will be running four sales motions instead of two for an extended period of time. Remember, it is *and*, not *or*. They will still be executing New + Renew selling for legacy Level 1 or 2 operating models and Land + Expand for their new Level 3 or 4 businesses.

How much experimentation a given supplier does in parallel inside separate teams or divisions in the near term will need to be traded against the simplicity of moving their whole go-to-market model to Land + Expand. Running in parallel is less disruptive to their next-quarter financials, but it will ultimately slow their progress in pivoting to B4B. We are working with a number of executive teams right now on how to think through that trade-off.

But the deciding vote will ultimately be cast by customers. They will be "voting with their feet" through the pace at which they move to new Level 3 and 4 suppliers. The key for suppliers is to accurately anticipate and plan for that transition. It is better that they learn Land + Expand selling one year too early rather than one year too late.

8 | Pivot 2: Adoption Services

THE SECOND PIVOT IS THE CREATION OF A NEW SERVICE OFFER called adoption services.

Adoption services are part of a class of services that we call optimize services. As we covered in Chapter 5, there are two service lines within this class, as shown in Figure 8.1.

Optimize and Outcome Services

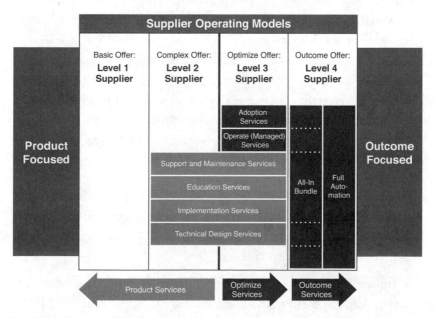

FIGURE 8.1 Optimize and Outcome Services

As you can see, adoption services are most likely to be found beginning at Level 3. It is a natural fit. This is because how the supplier adds value and how they recognize revenue begin to change at this level. At Levels 1 and 2, the customer assumes almost all of the responsibility for operating the product and achieving the business outcomes. But beginning at Level 3, the supplier's operating model starts to absorb some of those responsibilities. By either remotely operating the technology or guiding the practices of end users, the supplier becomes actively involved in ensuring that the products are functioning effectively and that the important advanced capabilities of the product are being used. As we argue in Chapter 10, this model can lead to significant improvements in overall ROI for the customer.

From the supplier's standpoint, ensuring that the products are successfully adopted becomes more than an altruistic objective. Beginning at Level 3 and continuing in Level 4, the revenue a supplier receives from its customers is increasingly tied to the successful consumption of the product. Although we have talked about consumption-based pricing models throughout the book, it is worth repeating that the risk of owning technology is rapidly shifting from customers to their suppliers. Pricing schemes commonly used at Levels 3 and 4 can already be seen heading in this direction. Even Level 2 suppliers are seeing customers and competitors exerting pressure on their traditional pricing models. Here are six summary statements about pricing pressures that we see playing out in the tech industry today which lead us to conclude that adoption services make economic sense for suppliers:

- OpEx spending is replacing CapEx spending.
- Unit prices are heading down because of competitive pressure.
- Customers want to pay only for what they use: Use more; pay more. Use less; pay less.
- If they don't use it or they don't like it, they want to stop paying. Although suppliers are currently trying to enforce large,

minimum commitments, customers are increasingly resisting them.

- Unit prices are shifting from single, fixed-price bundles to multiple tiers or optional add-ons. A common example is when SaaS prices move from a single per-user-per-month price to several options based on levels of functionality.
- Large-scale customers are talking to their strategic suppliers about gain-sharing arrangements.

In short, it seems that more and more every quarter, consumption equals revenue. Typically, at Levels 1 and 2, customers agree to purchase their products and services up front. The supplier only has to worry about customer satisfaction in order to preserve their potential for revenue in some future period. At Levels 3 and 4, all this changes. The supplier's current revenue is now dependent on how much each customer consumes each day. How fast, how well, how often, and how much customers consume will soon become four important questions facing a supplier. Once that observation becomes clear to the CEO of a high-tech or near-tech supplier, the very next question they ask is, "How do we make it go faster?" In *Consumption Economics*,[1] we alluded to the moment when a CEO realizes that the company must drive for faster results on these critical KPIs, and then realizes that he or she has no gas pedal.

Adoption services are a CEO's new gas pedal.

Let's define it a bit. Adoption services are project and annuity services designed to accelerate and optimize a customer's business outcome from technology by achieving widespread use of its capabilities.

Adoption services is not (necessarily) a separate service organization. It is a line of services that can be offered on top of existing organizational infrastructures within the suppler. Project-based adoption services can be offered by the existing professional services organization. Annuity-based adoption services can be offered by the existing customer support organization, both central support and field services. They can be offered to customers on a direct basis from the product supplier, or they can be offered through its channel of resellers.

The adoption services portfolio will develop over time, but there are three minimum offers:

- **Adoption Planning:** a project-based service offered by professional services designed to plan the optimal adoption of a new technology deployment. This plan will direct the adoption activities of both the supplier and the customer.

- **Consumption Monitoring:** an annuity service offered by the customer support organization designed to report to the customer on current adoption or utilization levels. This service reports on equipment activity levels for hardware and end-user adoption (EUA), feature or capability adoption, and volumes for software. Ideally, this reporting should trend actual results versus the intended results of the adoption plan.

- **Consumption Optimization:** an annuity service offered by the customer support organization (both central support and field services) designed to intervene with end users or with the technology itself to optimize a customer's business outcome through widespread use of its capabilities.

Adoption services should be engineered to follow a simple construct we call PIMO: plan, implement, monitor, and optimize. But more on PIMO in a minute.

Key Capabilities for Adoption Services

Like all elements of the transformation of supplier models to Levels 3 and 4, adoption services will require a mix of capabilities. Some already exist. Some are new.

The six capabilities listed in Figure 8.2 are new to most high-tech and near-tech service organizations. Let's look at them briefly.

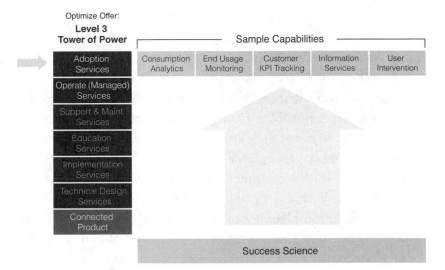

FIGURE 8.2 Sample Adoption Service Capabilities in the Level 3 Tower of Power

The tie-in to Success Science is absolutely critical to both the effectiveness and the efficiency of adoption services. In Chapter 5, we defined Success Science as a constant process, not a one-time project, which synthesizes multiple data and information inputs in a structured manner to articulate a solution's key success factors and the best practices to achieve them. Once understood, Success Science provides the sheet music that orchestrates the supplier delivery organization's reproduction of those conditions with as many customers as possible.

You can think of Success Science as the brain and adoption services as the arms and legs of a supplier's outcome-driven operating model. It should be the place where best practices for every single step of the customer life cycle are maintained. These best practices should be driving the design and execution of the adoption services portfolio. They should also be driving myriad practices at each individual customer. PTC's Best Practice Academy is a nice start on this concept. It doesn't just concern itself with teaching an employee of one of its manufacturing customers a few features; it also endeavors to teach them things such as assembly structure methodology best practices. By having this kind of content available, both the supplier's consultants and the customer's management can work together to get the optimum benefits from the software's great features.

A second important capability cuts across all three offers in the adoption services portfolio. Customer KPIs are the vital signs of their outcome. Many of these important KPIs will be identified in the Success Science process. But others may be unique or particularly important to that customer. They also may change over time. A supplier must have the capability to identify customers' KPIs as part of an adoption planning project, track their progress as part of the consumption monitoring service, and be able to improve them as part of the consumption optimization service. Doing this effectively and at scale depends on the robust data handshake that we cover in Chapter 9. It also relies on several internal product capabilities that many Level 1 and 2 products simply don't have. We believe that redirecting R&D activities to build these capabilities is hugely important to most every supplier we know.

End-user monitoring and intervention are two other essential capabilities most high-tech and near-tech products lack. Yet it is a common capability in B2C e-commerce. These give a whole new power to the operating model of Level 3 and 4 suppliers. In e-commerce, if a consumer has things in his or her shopping cart, hits the CHECKOUT button, and then doesn't complete the transaction, the retailer's website has a pop-up chat box appear to provide live assistance. Somehow, large online retailers can afford to do that 24/7 for millions of customers conducting low-value transactions. Yet inside many businesses today, highly skilled and compensated employees waste precious time struggling with mastering a new software feature, programming a new production run, or making copies of a complicated document. The math makes no sense. If suppliers could intervene for a fully burdened cost of $100 to get a $40,000-per-hour production line running an hour sooner, why aren't they? If a supplier can record a nearly free, 60-second YouTube video that saves a $200,000-a-year engineer 30 minutes on a computer-assisted design (CAD) project, why doesn't that supplier record it? Soon live video and remote operation will allow suppliers to actually do complex work for customers. Imagine needing 500 copies of a complex document from a high-end production print machine. Why not just hit a "Do it for me!" button on the machine, show the original document to the remote adoption services representative on a built-in webcam, and let them program the machine's operation remotely? With growing customer awareness of the high "slow-time" costs that come with employee end users struggling to adopt advanced capabilities, end-user monitoring and intervention are going to be welcome new capabilities.

Another emerging adoption service capability is in the area of information services. Stated simply, information services improve customer data or give that data added dimension. Suppliers could accomplish this by supplementing, cleaning, or analyzing customers' data. There are many suppliers offering excellent examples of information services. Eloqua, a marketing automation SaaS provider, offers an augmentation service called DemandBase that automatically adds key firmographic data to lead form submissions to build out the profile of a sales prospect. ServiceSource, a recurring revenue management SaaS provider, offers a data service option for pulling, cleaning, and enhancing renewal and subscription data for its Renew OnDemand customers. Philips Healthcare offers its hospital customers utilization services that measure and benchmark actual scanner performance, identifying improvement opportunities that can be used to set direction for department operation. GE Healthcare offers an information service called DoseWatch, which tracks, reports, and monitors the radiation dose delivered to patients. This is a critical activity that hospital staff used to do manually, which costs time and creates patient risk due to inaccuracies.

DoseWatch improves the hospital's performance, effectiveness, and safety. Information services such as these can be monetized separately or can be included as part of a larger adoption service offer.

The last of our example capabilities is one we would like to spend a little more time on. It has to do with the subject of analytics, specifically consumption analytics.

At TSIA, we are studying how big data analytics can be used to improve the efficiency of supplier services and improve the business outcomes of customers. We have organized our research framework into three simple tiers, as shown in Figure 8.3.

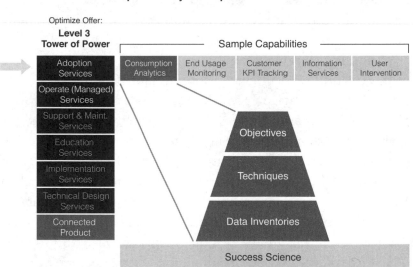

FIGURE 8.3 Consumption Analytics Capabilities Framework

The top layer of the framework is about establishing the analytic objectives. We have identified three broad objectives on which service organizations should focus their analytics:

- **Service Efficiency:** Analyze case information, plus asset signals, to optimize service delivery. Feed learnings to R&D to improve future serviceability of products.

- **Customer Adoption:** Analyze usage information, plus customer support requests, to optimize customer adoption of product capabilities. Feed learnings to R&D to improve future product designs.

- **Customer Business Outcomes:** Analyze customer success across the base; find differentiating practices and develop service offers to replicate them across the largest possible number of customers.

To pursue those objectives, we apply two classes of analytic techniques:

- **Descriptive Analytics:** These include basic reports and alerts for metrics, scores, and KPIs, combined with data reduction and customer segmentation techniques.

- **Predictive Analytics:** These include more advanced abilities such as model-driven scoring, A/B testing, multivariate models, and rule learning.

Finally, we have identified seven sources of data inventory:

- Product
- Environment
- Interactions
- Usage
- Process
- Customer
- Industry

By executing against this simple three-tiered structure, suppliers can mine the huge volumes of data being generated by connected products to improve customer outcomes and internal operating costs. If both sides can agree to a data-handshake strategy, the benefits can be enormous.

Consumption analytics, along with connected product and the data handshake, are the technical breakthroughs that will reinvent the customer-supplier partnership. Before now, even the most caring suppliers simply could not actively participate in improving customer outcomes on any kind of scale. They simply could not afford to have customer service reps calling up every end user of every customer every day to ask them if they needed any help. Before now, about the best they could afford to do was respond to in-bound assistance requests and send out customer satisfaction surveys. This was the economic limit of the partnering potential of Level 1 and Level 2 operating models. But now, a whole new world of partnership opportunities is opening up thanks to software and the Internet eating the world. Consumption analytics are a core capability to enable these possibilities. Real-time data and analytics will feed a scoring system that can measure the health of adoption and will target needed optimization activities.

Several Level 3 companies have begun their consumption analytics capabilities journey by developing an engagement model that predicts whether subscribers renew or don't renew. They identify certain "sticky" functionality that, once adopted, makes it highly likely that a particular customer will renew. Then, by monitoring the adoption levels of all customers on those key features at various points in time and comparing them to an ideal-state model, they can predict which customers need additional support. They can then execute prescribed customer outreach activities to remediate the adoption latency.

PIMO

In Chapter 5, we drew an analogy between the Tower of Power at Level 3 and the process that a hospital uses to optimize the likelihood of a positive outcome for a patient. We want to use that analogy again to illustrate how a high-tech or near-tech customer might experience adoption services during a deployment life cycle (see Figure 8.4).

PIMO – The Hospital "Tower of Power" Analogy

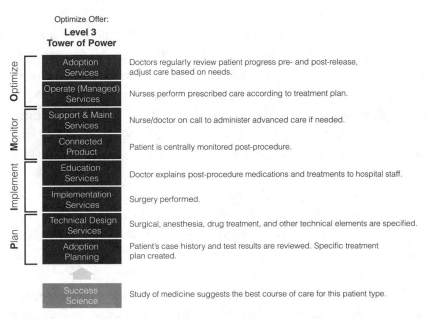

FIGURE 8.4 PIMO: The Tower of Power Analogy

PIMO is an acronym for plan, implement, monitor, and optimize. We know this is an obvious way for both suppliers and customers to think about the deployment of a technology solution. However, we argue that in Level 1 and 2 operating models, it is rarely done to its full potential.

In our hospital analogy, the plan phase would consist of both a technical plan for treatment that might specify the surgery, medications, and so on, as well as an overall treatment plan, which might specify the post-surgical care and lifestyle changes for the patient. The implement phase would include performing the actual procedure and educating the patient and recovery staff about results, findings, and required actions. In the monitor phase, what hospitals might call the recovery phase, the patient is closely monitored. Assistance is immediately available should post-procedure complications develop. Concurrently, the optimize phase begins

when prescribed treatment care is performed and changes in patient lifestyle are initiated. Doctors regularly review progress and
make adjustments as needed. Both hospital staff and the patient
may receive updated instructions from the doctor. The optimize
phase lasts as long as is required to achieve the desired outcome.
For a simple procedure, it may be a period of weeks. For a complex and critical procedure, the optimize phase may last a lifetime.

We think that this sequence is highly analogous to how technology deployments should be thought of. But because Level 1
and Level 2 suppliers have historically preferred to stay close to
their products, their involvement in this life cycle has been intentionally limited. As indicated by the black boxes in Figure 8.4, these
suppliers have leaned toward activities tied directly to the product,
not to the customer. They offer services to design the technical solution, implement it, train on it, and keep it operational.
What they have not typically done is to prepare the customer's
internal organization for success, to manage and/or operate the
technology, or to ensure successful outcomes. This gap is what
optimize services are meant to address.

At Level 3, this means that the three new adoption service
offers join operate (managed) services to provide far more supplier engagement in the full life cycle. So now, in the:

- **Plan Phase**, adoption planning joins technical design services
  and implementation planning.
- **Monitor Phase**, consumption monitoring joins remote system uptime monitoring.
- **Optimize Phase**, consumption optimization and operation
  services join customer service activities such as support and
  field service.

We believe these will be natural additions to the service portfolio
for companies at Level 3. At Level 4, these same activities should
also take place either as part of an all-in bundle or, ideally, as part

of the "full-automation" offer. We think the adoption planning service is the low-hanging fruit of the three adoption service offers. By working closely with the technical solutions architect, the result is a plan to develop the complete business solution, to smooth the edges of complexity on both sides, and to make the outcome frictionless. Rather than "implement first, optimize later," customers and suppliers can work on both concurrently. The adoption plan can identify the good business processes that the customer wants to amplify and the bad processes they want to engineer out using process charts or consultants. This service should also select the best deployment plan, identify key KPIs, and determine which party is responsible for each. The adoption plan can also chart the key functions that are critical to important job roles for the customer so that consumption optimization can focus on driving them.

Organizing for Adoption Services

As we have stressed repeatedly to our high-tech and near-tech member companies, building out new organizations every time a new service line comes along is not a winning strategy for a maturing industry facing declining prices and tightening margins. Adoption services provide the perfect opportunity to break the cycle. As we said, we believe there will be both project-based and annuity-based adoption services. There are already organizations at both delivery modes within most tech suppliers; no need for more.

What is needed is for suppliers to chart a course toward a converged services model. This approach could reduce their total service delivery costs across all their service lines by 10% to 20%, or more, while simultaneously improving their effectiveness. It will also facilitate the capability to create virtual, cross-service-line teams that can focus on a single customer. From a customer standpoint, these are exactly what they need and want from a supplier. For most Level 2 suppliers today, service focus = service organization. This means that customers, or third-party systems integrators, are left to act as the general contractor. They must work with all the service "subs" inside the supplier's organization. They talk to separate service salespeople, have separate "go-to" contact points. It makes no sense. But suppliers don't often organize their service delivery from a customer perspective; they organize their service delivery to maximize financial command and control. That was both understandable and common in the era of Levels 1 and 2 operating models. But we don't think it is right for B4B.

Generally speaking, we think that the current professional services organization should house the adoption planning offer. We think the current customer (or tech) support organization should house the consumption monitoring offer. Finally, we think the current customer support and field services organizations should house the consumption optimization offer. Each of the existing organizations will need to add new capabilities to their repertoire. We have covered a few of those new capabilities in this chapter.

Adoption services are also offers that product companies might elect to turn over to their reseller channel, at least for some customer segments. There are many good reasons for considering this approach. Many supplier executives may prefer this because it reduces internal complexity. Others may need the resellers to offer their core products and, especially in an era of OpEx pricing models, they would like to entice them with other ways of making money. It gives their channel partners a new revenue stream to supplement their eroding product-attached service revenue. Some product companies are taking a similar tact with operate or managed service offers. However, there are two challenges that must be addressed in order to make resellers successful in adoption services.

The first and most challenging is the access to customer data and personnel. Both consumption monitoring and consumption optimization are dependent on constant visibility into customer utilization. As we have discussed, this may make some customer executives uncomfortable. In those cases, it is going to require the product company to put in place lots of safeguards and agreements in order to ease those concerns. The challenge may be even greater for a reseller, particularly a smaller one. Customers will need a lot of convincing that a small reseller can actually implement and operate a complex data protection and end-user intervention program. We believe that this is a problem in which the product company is in the best position to solve for its resellers.

The second challenge is the link to Success Science. The "smarts" that enable all three adoption services should be developed and maintained through the Success Science process we described in Chapter 5. That is going to be a labor- and skills-intensive process. It may not be practical for the reseller to build this capability for itself. Once again, we think the product company must come to its aid.

Both of these challenges can be boiled down to a simple question: Who puts up the capital to get resellers into the adoption services business? We think the best approach is for the product companies to build an adoption service SaaS application and then grant or sell access to its resellers.

Inside that application, resellers would find the tools, frameworks, and best practices created by the product company's Success Science team. This will enable the resellers to build their adoption planning offer without needing to fund a Success Science process themselves. On top of that, we think the product company must build a consumption monitoring and optimization engine. Inside that engine would be the data-handshake utilities. We think that in most cases it makes sense for product companies to handle the complex data security and access issues directly with customers. Their sheer size and credibility may increase the customer's confidence. Last, this engine should have all the functionality needed for the reseller to operate its consumption monitoring and optimization adoption service offers. Suppliers would build it and may operate some aspects of it. Resellers would have a license to use it in whole or in part. This application, built and owned by the supplier, puts resellers "in the business" of adoption services. We think many product companies will elect to charge their reseller partner for this application.

This approach overcomes the capital limitations that many smaller resellers may face. It means that only one Success Science and consumption engine needs to be built, not one at every reseller. We think it has the best chance for success. We believe that customers will be more comfortable with that approach and that resellers will be more successful as a result. For the product company, it is an alluring addition to attract resellers to its core product offer.

As we said, if the product company elects to deliver adoption services directly, the organizational approach to who builds and manages these offers should be straightforward. What will be far more important to consider is how to manage the very close dependencies between adjacent organizations within the supplier. We think there will be six critical operational adjacencies that successful adoption service organizations will face:

- **Adoption Services → Land + Expand Selling:** to get adoption planning projects attached to the land sale and to execute on expand selling opportunities, i.e., micro upsell and cross-sell transactions (the little dots)

- **Adoption Services → Professional Services:** to make sure that the technical design services and implementation project plan consider and coordinate with the adoption planning project plan

- **Adoption Services → Education Services:** to receive targeted education content that can be delivered on a just-in-time basis to end users

- **Adoption Services → Marketing**: to drive targeted feature promotions at selected end users based on both known best adoption practices and/or according to the adoption plan

- **Adoption Services → Customer Service**: to be able to route inbound "how-to" cases from customer support to the consumption optimization team and to utilize field service personnel if on-site consumption optimization activities are required

- **Adoption Services → Success Science:** to receive its best adoption practices and to feed data and results for further research

The Skills Gap

One of the biggest challenges facing suppliers in this pivot is a slightly ironic one. Because they have always preferred to stay close to their products rather than close to the outcome, they have staffed accordingly. This means that suppliers are loaded with technical experts in their service organization who have deep knowledge of the product. They know how to troubleshoot it, to debug it, to customize it, and to fix it. In fact, nearly everyone is an engineer of some sort or another. They have impressive technical certifications and have been thoroughly trained on the product's design and ideal operation.

But they may not have any idea how to get a business outcome from it.

Obviously, mastering a mechanical near-tech product does not require a deep knowledge of the industry it is being used in or the business processes surrounding it. It usually just needs to be installed properly. But the more software that is involved, the more chances there are for suboptimal utilization. That's not because it is broken. It is because the customer's employees are not taking full advantage of its advanced capabilities. That might be easy to remedy with a little bit of just-in-time education. But often the issue is more complex. There may be so many features that the customers don't really know which ones are best to master. They don't know which advanced capabilities might best benefit them based on their industry, their job role, or their end-customers' requirements. They may not know what the best-practice business process is that should be implemented to maximize its usefulness.

So there is actually a skills gap on both sides of the equation. The supplier is loaded with technical experts who know the product, and customers are loaded with people who know their job and industry well but who may not know how to map the product's features to it in the optimal way.

Adoption service experts would ideally have both. So how do we solve this? In two ways: The first is that the Success Science team must take on this mapping assignment as a key deliverable. It must provide consumption road maps and training that the adoption service employees can learn and use. The second is that the supplier needs to stop hiring service employees from other tech companies and start hiring them from the industries they serve. Suppliers have plenty of existing training material on the products. They do not have plenty of training material on the industries they serve or the business processes within them. They should hire for that experience and should train for the product knowledge.

This is the fastest path to building a nucleus of consumption optimization expertise. Having industry experience in customer markets is almost a requirement for Success Science engineers. It will also be prized background for adoption service staff.

What Adoption Services Mean to Customers

As we mentioned, we think that customers will be excited to have their suppliers more engaged in delivering optimal business outcomes from their technology investments. Improved adoption of existing technology could lead to significant improvements in revenue or lowering of costs. The payoff should be clear and measurable. Demonstrating returns in such a precise manner is how suppliers should explain the virtues of adoption services. They should be able to point out to customers how these new services will improve specific KPIs that matter to them.

In turn, customers must agree to the grand bargain. They must also be willing to engage in adoption planning side by side with the supplier's adoption consultants. Although the adoption plan will direct the activities on both the supplier and the customer side, it is primarily what happens on the customer side that will determine the speed and scope of the outcome. This means that managers must be engaged in the plan and held accountable for its execution. If it is application software, they must take the time to plan ideal consumption road maps for key employee job roles. End users must also be brought into that process. Obviously, the difficulty in developing and executing the plan will be directly tied to the amount of end-user software in the offer. The more end-user features, the more important the adoption plan.

Adoption services are real. They are happening today. Salesforce.com is using consumption analytics to create engagement dashboards; Apple is doing targeted, feature-specific marketing; Best Buy's Geek Squad is producing and delivering targeted, two-minute "how-to" videos; and Taleo is monitoring customer KPIs and intervening with end users to help improve them. We already mentioned how GE and Philips are actively involved in helping hospitals improve safety and be more efficient. All of this is really happening. But no one has put it all together. No one has really built the Frankenstein's monster model that is possible today. Now is the time.

For Suppliers, Adoption Services Will Soon Be Essential

There are three final reasons why suppliers at every level should embrace adoption services. And they are all important ones. The first is that the brief history of Level 3 and 4 business models has already shown us that it is very important to diversify a supplier's revenue. The simple XaaS price list is prone to commoditization and prices wars. If suppliers have not found other services to monetize that add value to customers, then they are more exposed to this risk. We know of some cloud service offers that have faced as many as six price cuts in a single year. By standing up valuable new adoption service offers, suppliers can add more legs to their revenue stool. That creates a more stable base.

The second motivation is going to be competitive. If two suppliers are competing for the business of a large customer and only one offers these services, who do you think will win? Although we acknowledge that few suppliers truly offer all these services today, we predict that they will rapidly become table stakes in many large deals. This will give a competitive advantage to suppliers who host the customer's technology, have developed their data handshake, and don't have as many technical support cases to burden their resources. This is why SaaS has decided advantages over other architectures. Those new table stakes won't make Level 2 companies happy, but we think the market won't be very patient with excuses like architectural limitations that keep them from offering things such as consumption monitoring or consumption optimization.

The third reason, as we mentioned in Chapter 3, is because of the growing evidence that traditional Level 2 service offers, such as customer support, maintenance, and professional services, will soon be growth challenged. Many Level 2 suppliers are relying on product-attached services growth and profits to offset declining fundamentals in their product businesses. Without them, their overall financial picture weakens considerably. We think optimize services is the answer to their problem. We have already documented the rapid growth rates of operate (managed) services. We expect similar growth rates for adoption services. Suppliers must move their service portfolio to the right, away from their products and toward their customer's outcome. While these two offers are natural activities beginning at Level 3, they can also be beneficial to Level 2 suppliers and their customers. Without them, Level 2 suppliers may lose out to Level 3 competitors. Without them, Level 2 suppliers might be unable to offset the erosion in their current service portfolio. Without them, Level 2 suppliers might be in trouble.

9 | Pivot 3: The Data Handshake

Aт THE END OF THE DAY, ENGAGING IN LEVEL 3 AND LEVEL 4 operating models profitably resolves down to one enabling capability: consumption analytics. With this capability, suppliers can help customers achieve unprecedented business outcomes from their employees and equipment. Without it, such assistance is simply not possible; it's too full of friction and labor.

Obviously, the analytics are dependent on data. And unfortunately, we seem to have another Goldilocks problem on that topic. We often hear Level 1 and 2 suppliers complain that they don't have enough usage data. We hear Level 3 and 4 suppliers, such as SaaS companies, say they are overwhelmed by it. We hear some customers say they won't allow any of their data out in the cloud and won't let suppliers connect to their on-premise products. We hear others say that they feel vulnerable because they are completely reliant on a cloud XaaS provider to handle their data. They may nervously have their financials, their new products designs, or the identity of their big deals for the next quarter all in the hands of a Level 3 or Level 4 supplier whom they have never met.

So why would we devote an entire pivot to just this one area? Compared to Land + Expand selling or adoption services, behavioral data or consumption analytics might seem like a pretty small topic. But we view consumption analytics as a crown jewel that will differentiate the winners from the losers in executing everything else we've talked about in this book. On the back of rapidly decreasing compute and storage costs, top suppliers are fundamentally transforming both their own operating models and the basis of competition in their industries. Suppliers simply cannot get from Levels 1 or 2 to Levels 3 and 4 without this new capability.

The Data Handshake

So if you've gotten this far in the book, you are intrigued by the power of B4B. In the B2C world, the analytics train has already left the station. Apple knows more about music consumption than does any musician or music company. Amazon knows more about shopping than does any traditional retailer. Google knows more about the topics people are interested in than does any news organization. Facebook knows more about the people in our lives than we do. LinkedIn knows what company you might work for next before you think about making a change. How? These suppliers have engineered a data handshake with their consumer customers. Now we need one in B4B.

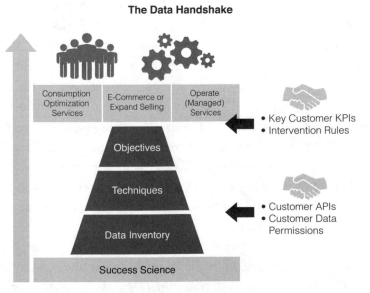

The Data Handshake

FIGURE 9.1 The Data Handshake

Although certainly more complex than the exchanges that take place in the B2C world, the data handshake that is needed between business customers and their Level 3 and 4 suppliers (shown in Figure 9.1) is going to be conceptually very similar. In essence, the data handshake represents a set of mutual agreements between a supplier and its customers for data sharing, monitoring, and usage intervention with either employees or machines.

In Chapter 8, we talked about the critical consumption analytics capability that a supplier must master. We identified seven sources of data inventory to feed their analytic techniques:

- Product
- Environment
- Interactions
- Usage
- Process
- Customer
- Industry

The point of origin for virtually all of that data is the equipment or the customer—specifically, the customer's employee end users. They are the ones who are using the technology product. They turn the equipment on and off, program it to perform functions, select features, and conduct transactions. Somehow, some way, those actions and the resulting data that they originate need to make their way to the supplier. There the supplier can apply various techniques to turn that data into useful and actionable insight. This insight then triggers actions that benefit both the customer and the supplier. Because these insights are linked to the supplier's business processes within their consumption monitoring, optimization, and operate service organizations, the supplier can efficiently intervene to help optimize the customer's outcome.

But this cycle, shown in Figure 9.2, means that two things must be agreed to: what data will be shared and what actions will be taken.

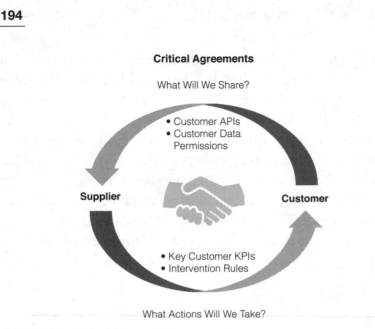

Critical Agreements

What Will We Share?

Supplier

- Customer APIs
- Customer Data Permissions

Customer

- Key Customer KPIs
- Intervention Rules

What Actions Will We Take?

FIGURE 9.2 Critical Agreements

Without these critical agreements, the true power of Level 3 and Level 4 operating models never even begins.

The Supplier Side of Big Consumption Data

Leading Level 3 and Level 4 suppliers are already harvesting user behavioral data from their installed bases and turning it into profitable insights for themselves and their customers. This has been particularly true of the early SaaS companies. Their cloud-deployment models and multi-tenant architectures have enabled them to heavily instrument all aspects of the behavior of all users. For some, this has been taken down to the individual mouse click of every end user. They can build this behavioral tracking natively into their solutions. These SaaS companies can then analyze patterns across very large user communities, extract the specific user behaviors that lead to the fastest time-to-customer business value, and use this knowledge to differentiate themselves from their competitors. They can also run their adoption-led expand selling model with facts—and not just gut instincts. They know what the next module that a given customer or even a department within a customer is going to need based on the patterns observed in other customers—somewhat like Amazon knowing what the next book is that a particular consumer will want to read.

Suppliers that have grown up in the traditional CapEx models of Levels 1 and 2 have been much slower to move. They have not yet made the investments to instrument their products down to the user level. They have not yet built a flexible data aggregation model in which behavioral data are aggregated behind customers' firewalls in some deployments and on suppliers' servers in others. They have not yet adjusted their customer contracts to reflect who gets what rights to what data. They have not built out a road map of the behavioral consumption analytics that will maximize customer business value for their solutions. Some suppliers have made a small step toward solution monitoring and instrumentation, but mainly for their own interests. For example, many Level 1 and 2 suppliers have placed "collectors" in their customers' environments for installed-base management. These systems track the deployment of that supplier's component products, including serial numbers, software versions, operating status, and so on. The suppliers then use this information to ensure that every piece of their equipment is covered by a maintenance contract. Although this adds some value for customers, it ensures that they are "covered" for ongoing maintenance; however, it does nothing to instrument the actual usage of the solution. It is becoming increasingly clear that this slow progress toward becoming a big consumption data expert is putting these suppliers at a significant disadvantage relative to their IaaS, PaaS, and SaaS competitors. They must speed up their progress.

The Customer Side of Big Consumption Data

Many customers have already figured out the strategic value of behavioral data analysis capabilities for themselves and have been investing in them for years. They are capturing and internally analyzing the consumption behavior of their employees as they interact with the high-tech and near-tech solutions they have deployed. Some might even track the behavior of their strategic partners' employees who have access to their systems. These customers are then leveraging the insights from behavioral analytics to streamline and improve their operations.

This notion is not new. Way back in 2004, for example, UPS had Symbol Technologies build 90,000 advanced rugged mobile computers for its global delivery fleet. Given that every UPS driver carried this device at all times, the GPS within the device enabled UPS to track the specific driving and walking route that each driver took when delivering each day's packages. UPS was able to analyze this behavioral data relative to the best possible route and to identify inefficiencies in an individual driver's actions. Based on these insights, UPS was able to give drivers specialized training to help them get their work done with a minimum amount of fatigue, minimum risk of injury, and maximum on-time performance. There are many such examples of this kind of optimization activity across almost every industry.

But usually these activities were conducted internally. The original consumption data that enabled the optimization never went outside the customers' firewalls. But that meant that customers paid the whole bill. They paid to have the capability developed, and they paid internal staff to conduct the analysis and implement the recommendations. In Level 3 and Level 4 operating models, suppliers take on those development costs. They can deliver the same kinds of benefits to customers for a tiny fraction of doing it all in-house. However, this means that customers must agree to let the data leave their control in some form.

We think that the question of what form that data transfer takes will be a critical one with which both sides will wrestle. What options can suppliers present to the customer to assuage their concerns? Can they anonymize the data? Can they aggregate the data? Can they segment and separate the data? Then, for whatever data the customer is willing to share, how will suppliers protect it, archive it, or dispose of it?

When customers are uncomfortable with having some or all of their raw data out of their direct command and control, we can imagine an arrangement in which customers provide their Level 3 and 4 suppliers with insider access to carefully selected behavioral and consumption data of their employees on a "one-to-many" basis. This will enable their Level 3 and 4 suppliers to add the maximum amount of business value for them in the least amount of time. The customer could achieve this best-of-both-worlds state by engineering two sets of APIs (application programming interfaces): a "public" set that many of its suppliers could connect to, and a larger "private" set available only to a select few strategic partners.

This difference between public and private APIs has some history behind it. Decades ago, Walmart took on this strategy with its supply chain. Walmart wanted to enable all of its suppliers to be more efficient in ensuring that they maintained just enough inventory in its stores at all times. It was focused on maximizing inventory "turns," that is, its sell-through revenue versus its inventory levels. To do so, it made available to all suppliers its basic views of its point-of-sale (POS) data so that each consumer products company and wholesale distributor could better plan their actions to ensure Walmart was never out of stock and never had excess inventory. In parallel, Walmart was an early investor in business interlock technology called EDI, or electronic data interchange. With its best suppliers, Walmart made available a much more granular view of its sell-through data and even tied its ordering, receiving, and inventory management systems directly into those of its strategic suppliers. Procter & Gamble (P&G) was an early example. This enabled those strategic suppliers to add even more value in areas like vendor-managed inventories. That is, P&G actually managed the inventories in Walmart's distribution centers and the merchandising in Walmart's stores for certain categories of its products. If you think about it, this is an exact parallel of a high-tech or near-tech supplier stepping up to managed services or adoption services of their products in B4B.

In return for providing data, customers can demand that their suppliers share the behavioral data and analytics with them as part of their B4B relationship. This is really what the consumption monitoring service is all about. So think about the data handshake as a two-way street: customers sharing access to their raw data and suppliers repaying them with optimal ROI from their solutions.

Key Capabilities for the Data Handshake

There are many challenges facing Level 3 and 4 suppliers. There are technical issues such as security, multi-tenancy, and latency. But as we said, success at these levels is about much more than remote hosting or subscription pricing. Taking advantage of the power of these new operating models requires many new capabilities. Here are two more that are tied to successfully utilizing consumption analytics to improve business outcomes.

New Customer Agreements
The potential that lives inside B4B is exciting to consider. But it will be all for naught if customers will not agree to provide the enabling data or to allow suppliers to intervene with its employee end users or the product itself.

In the world of B2C e-commerce, suppliers rely on strong brands and high consumer confidence to earn their customers' data trust. They supplement their own brands by earning third-party trustmarks such a TRUSTe, obtaining security certifications from familiar sources such as McAfee, or by linking to separate payment entities such as PayPal. These encourage consumers to part with critical data such as credit card numbers and home addresses. Consumers are also given opt-out options. They can elect to not house cookies or to not have credit card numbers stored. The bottom line is that leading B2C websites find a way to reach data handshakes with their consumer customers. Level 3 and Level 4 suppliers must find a way to do the same with their business customers.

These agreements will address both of the critical topics we identified in Figure 9.2. They will delineate what data will be shared and how the process will work. The agreement may also define what KPIs the customer wants tracked by that supplier. Last, the agreement must identify what intervention actions—either with technology or with end users—the supplier is authorized to perform. Although we think that this is a good standard practice for all customer-supplier partnerships, it is particularly essential at Levels 3 and 4. This agreement gives both parties a common understanding of when, where, and how the operating model of the supplier will touch the customer's operating model. It frames in the supplier's value proposition and protects both sides from potential legal or expectation conflicts. It may even govern and regulate which kinds of fee-based end-user consumption are commercially preapproved and which are not.

There is no doubt that the scope of these agreements will vary widely. Some customers may not even require one from certain suppliers in certain roles. In other cases, such agreements will be central to the overall partnership agreement. In any case, being able to negotiate these successfully will be an important capability for suppliers.

The R&D Balancing Act

Level 1 and 2 suppliers rightly focus on product features. At Levels 3 and 4, they have a second focus: the service platform. Throughout this book, we have talked about all the great things that suppliers at this level can do with their operating model. But doing all those great things profitably and at scale requires that suppliers sit on top of a powerful platform of technology.

The bottom line is this: No algorithmically derived insight will make a difference if suppliers cannot efficiently interlock it back into their business. By this, we mean changing what a supplier's personnel, process, and technology do and when they do it. That could be changing which subsequent module the expand sales team focuses on with a specific customer. It could also be what adoption service is launched for a specific customer at a specific point in its adoption of a solution. We have already talked about how a solution might need to be engineered to allow in-the-workflow suggestions and commerce. The platform will also need new consumption dashboards to see the status of the customer's progress toward maximum business value.

None of these is a "feature." These are a whole second thought. Beginning at Level 3, the suppliers' R&D teams don't just have one thing to keep them up at night; they have two. They must keep their features competitive *and* keep their operating platform effective. In the SaaS world, that may all be one huge software labyrinth with customer end users and supplier service employees accessing the same applications from different angles. In the world of connected but on-premise equipment, the end customer may never actually touch the platform; instead, he or she may just touch the technology product that is talking with the platform.

In any case, this service platform represents the business process interlock that sits between the enabling data and a successful outcome-driven operating model. R&D must either acquire much more funding to be able to support both activities or, more realistically, develop a higher bar for new feature additions. They must ask the hard questions about whether they really need to add feature number 1,344. Or are 1,343 features enough? In order to balance the new demand for far greater involvement of R&D resources into the construction and development of the operating model platform against the constant stream of new feature requests, R&D must become more judicious in their decisions. Adding even more pressure on them is the growing need to engineer out much of the current product complexity that customers are rebelling against.

All in all, building, negotiating, and operating the data handshake—and the platform it runs on—is harder than it sounds.

Organizing to Make the Data Handshake Pay Off

For most suppliers and customers, the actions required are new. They are "off the road map" from the existing strategy of either organization. Therefore, the right way to get started is likely a Center of Excellence (COE). In the case of suppliers, that COE may be their new Success Science team. If the customer plans to keep its data in-house and build its own adoption services organization, the customer may house the data and analytics as a COE within its existing IT or operations organization. In any case, a special-purpose organization meant to work across all other business units and functions may achieve the most substantial progress in the shortest time.

This type of COE is where a supplier will vest the responsibility to work across every product line, engineering team, sales region, and customer segment to develop and execute the strategy described earlier. The COE will need the direct sponsorship of the CEO, as they are going to have to use some "silver bullets" to get things done. This could mean working with engineering to prioritize deep instrumentation of user behavior above speeds, feeds, features, and functionality in the next major product release or technology deployment. It could also mean working with sales leadership to rewrite its sales methodology to shift from fact-free sales targeting to fact-based sales targeting. It might also mean working with legal advisors to rewrite standard contract terms and conditions to cover the data handshake described earlier. It almost certainly means substantial investments in incremental data storage and analytic tools to power your platform.

This type of COE must also win the war for talent among data scientists. Data scientists are going to be as in demand in the next five years as user experience engineers have been in the last five. There are going to be shortages. A supplier's COE will need to take a global approach to tap into the best data scientists regardless of their country of residence or education.

The COE approach is not unprecedented in this context. GE is becoming the clear leader in what it calls the Industrial Internet using this exact organizational model. They formed their software COE two years ago. This organization has jump-started a $150 billion, 110-year-old company's leverage of granular operational and behavioral data to achieve breakthrough economics for its customers. It is optimizing both the performance of the GE assets its customers have purchased as well as the operation of those assets by the employees of GE's customers. It is doing this across multiple industries, including aviation, rail, health care, oil and gas, and energy. It is doing an incredible job of winning the war for talent. If fact, its COE has expanded to 500 people in 24 months and is on track to hit 1,000 people in 2014. In short, the COE organizational approach has put GE on the map as an analytics powerhouse in the industries it serves in a very short time. Customers and suppliers alike would do well to study what GE has achieved and replicate its COE model.

So we have covered a lot of ground in the three pivots. We think these are all actionable and urgent conversations that should be taking place inside progressive suppliers and their customers. We want to end our discussion by talking about what these trends really mean for technology markets. We would like you to ask yourself: "Is your market really heading into the new era of B4B?"

10 | Crossing the Line

IT'S JUST A LINE ON A PIECE OF PAPER, THAT'S ALL. THE HARD LINE that separates Level 2 from Level 3.

Ask yourself, if you were the CEO of some new start-up supplier today in your industry and you wanted to disrupt the large incumbents, which operating model would you choose to build? After all, you would have a clean sheet of paper. You could build whatever kind of company you wanted!

From what our friends in the venture capital community are telling us, there are many Level 3 and Level 4 suppliers baking in the oven right now. Yet the truth is that Level 2 suppliers still dominate the landscape. This is especially true in larger, more established tech sectors. For them, the sheet of paper is not clean, and the choice to cross that line is not so simple. They are expected to deliver both short-term profits and long-term growth while they stare at the "fish problem," discussed in Chapter 6, that is sitting between these expectations.

Among customers, the hard line also represents challenges. Having suppliers with Level 3 and Level 4 operating models means that they must choose the grand bargain. They must begin to actively dismantle or reassign some of their internal operating capabilities in order to pay for suppliers' new services and simultaneously increase their ROI to the CFO. Usually this means reducing headcount.

So, on both sides of the great divide, hard decisions must be made about whether to cross that line. As the English rock band The Clash famously asked, "Should I stay, or should I go?"

Will There Be a New Normal?

When we first started talking about the decision with supplier execs several years ago, the need for operating and business model transformation was less clear. There were many reasons to believe that Level 1 suppliers could keep on with their frictionless model of make, sell, and ship. Most Level 2 suppliers also felt that their current operating model (shown in Figure 10.1) was their permanent one.

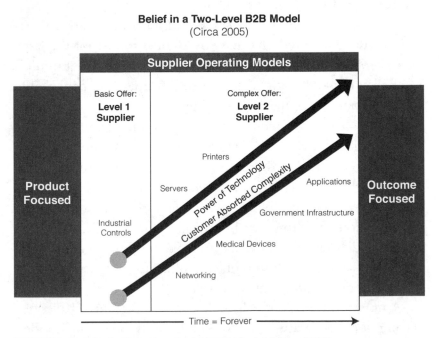

FIGURE 10.1 Belief in a Two-Level B2B Model (circa 2005)

For suppliers at that time, investing in R&D to build ever-increasing product power by adding more features while offering a growing portfolio of product services seemed like the proven path to *both* short-term profits and long-term growth. On the opposite side, customers had long accepted that they were the ones who needed to absorb the complexity that went along with tech and translate it into business outcomes. Although there was talk about improving the internal efficiency of organizations such as IT or operations, there was little talk about eliminating whole parts of them. That relatively stable, decades-long period was one in which management on both sides of the great divide was comfortable. All descendants of Patterson's B2B vision knew what everyone's role was and how each side of the Level 1 and Level 2 partnership was going to operate. While there was a small number of interesting new-model tech companies on the periphery, they seemed confined to SMB markets. In general, Level 1 and Level 2 partnership models were dominant.

Today, the level of discussion is much more serious and the actions being taken are more urgent. We don't think many executives on either side today would disagree that Level 3 and 4 operating models are viable, not just for SMBs, but for large enterprises as well.

But how far will it go? Are Level 3 and Level 4 supplier models just niche opportunities, or are they going to become the "new normal." Although it will certainly be the case that most suppliers will be in the "*and*, not *or*" situation of operating different models for different product markets for many years, the question of how big a bet to place on Levels 3 and 4—and when—is crucial.

If you are a senior executive of a high-tech or near-tech supplier, you are probably already facing these decisions. If you are a top IT, operations, or manufacturing executive on the customer side, you must decide how much and how soon you can depend on those suppliers to play new roles in your partnerships. Collectively, executives on both sides must decide for themselves: What is going to happen here? So we would like to end the book by assessing where many tech markets are going to go, not just based on our conclusions, but also on yours.

To pursue this topic together, we ask you to consider whether you agree or disagree with some of the core assertions of B4B:

1. New Level 1 offers are usually innovative, but often are in basic forms. They may be perfect for simple applications or individual end users. However, many of them are not yet sophisticated enough to be adopted by large enterprise customers.

2. Level 2 is where offers become industrial enough and flexible enough for large enterprises to be able to adopt and standardize them. Moving from Level 1 to Level 2 is usually the biggest single period of power growth for the product.

3. At Level 3, there can be some additional power added to the offer through active supplier involvement in daily product operating and adoption roles. Although the Level 3 offer is more powerful, the steepness of the power growth curve is less than when moving from Level 1 to 2.

4. At Level 4, customers may have to make some compromises to their normal expectations of a highly customized product in order to let the supplier de-risk the offer and ease complexity.

If you generally agree with these assertions, then you are probably OK with drawing an Offer Power Line (the product plus the services) on the B4B construct that looks something like that shown in Figure 10.2.

A couple of examples might help to illustrate the pattern. Think about the history of CRM software. In the early 1990s, Act! was the leading contact management software application for a salesperson's PC. But it took Siebel in the mid-1990s to make industrial-strength Level 2 CRM software. By 2008, salesforce.com had moved CRM to an industrial-strength Level 3 offer. Then think about how it has worked in a completely different near-tech market. Take an industrial product such as commercial HVAC. At Level 1, heating/air-conditioning units could control the temperature of a room, but it took Level 2 building

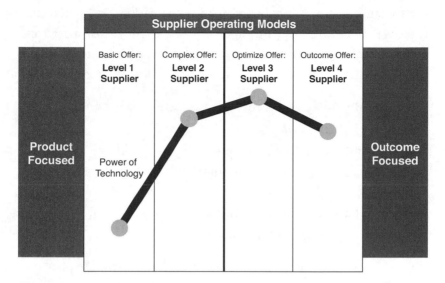

FIGURE 10.2 B4B Belief System

management systems to give owners the power to control their utility costs. Now "smart building" managed services providers are taking this industry to Level 3 by offering to actively manage these systems, improving their energy efficiency while also reducing on-site labor costs.

As we said, there are precious few Level 4 examples today. AWS and Rackspace are getting really close. Some tech sectors may never get to that point. But as some do, we believe the customer will need to adopt the supplier's way of doing things. The solutions they offer might not be quite as customized or sophisticated as their old Level 2 or 3 solutions were. The customer may not have quite as much control over how detailed processes work. They may even have to give up a few features. But in exchange, Level 4 customers may have far fewer headaches, far less risk, and far lower costs. This is exactly the trade-off going on today as a growing number of large enterprise CIOs are piloting AWS as a cloud storage supplier for non-mission-critical data.

If you can generally agree to the shape of that Offer Power Line (or something that approximates it in your market) in Figure 10.2, then we can move on to considering a second set of assertions. These relate to the complexity typically facing customers at the four levels. See how much you agree with these statements:

1. Customer-managed complexity at Level 2 is the highest of all levels.

2. A Level 3 offer begins to provide some relief to customer-managed complexity from supplier offers such as managed services or remote hosting.

3. A Level 4 offer, at least in theory, could drop customer-managed complexity dramatically.

If you generally agree with these assertions, then you are probably OK with adding a second line to the belief system diagram so that it might look something like what is shown in Figure 10.3.

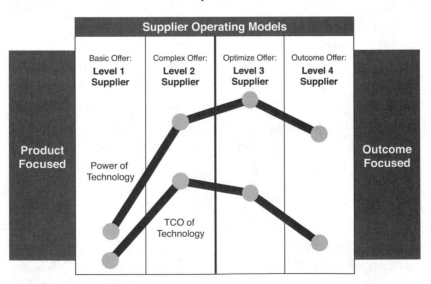

FIGURE 10.3 B4B Belief System

Together, these simple lines begin to bring the true potential of new B4B operating models into clear view. Although they may not provide the same gain in raw power that occurs when tech products move to Level 2, they represent the potential for something at least as important: better ROI (see Figure 10.4).

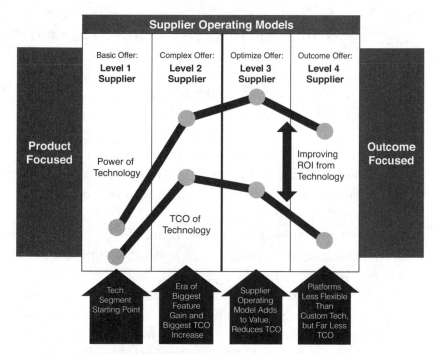

FIGURE 10.4 The ROI of B4B

We believe that many tech customers are shifting their focus from owning the most technology to extracting the most ROI from it. B4B offers a way to frame that journey for both the customers who want to experience it and the suppliers who want to deliver it. Suppliers' individual drawings of their product and/or markets will be unique. Likewise, customers may have different shapes to their lines in different categories of their tech spending.

But, importantly, we don't think the basic message of these lines will change.

The basic message is this: Level 2 suppliers may have offered the most rapid growth in the power of technology at Level 2, but it is Level 3 and Level 4 suppliers who may now offer the most rapid growth in customer ROI. That is how they will compete and, when ROI is the customer's priority in the decision, how they will win. Widening that gap between the power of technology and the total cost of ownership (TCO) is what every supplier at Levels 3 and 4 is banking on today to disrupt their incumbent Level 2 competitors. This is true whether they are a start-up or an established market leader making the transition.

The hard line that separates Level 2 from Level 3 is not only a line that changes the operating model of a supplier; it is also a line that changes how customers think. It will affect who they choose and why. It may lead them to sacrifice certain features for the confidence of a solid, dependable return on their investment. If they are willing to engage in the grand bargain of reducing in-house expenses, they may go from being alleged cost centers to proven profit centers. It is a simply irresistible proposition for customers. We recently heard one CIO say, "Eighty percent of the functionality at 50% of the total cost is exactly what I want." Customers are making explicit decisions on a category-by-category basis of where they still prioritize product innovation and where good-enough tech at a lower TCO is the perfect option. To many suppliers' dismay, more and more customers are switching more and more categories of spending from the former to the latter.

When this moment happens—when the hard line is crossed and the possible becomes reality—does anyone have a choice? When Level 3 and Level 4 supplier models begin offering much higher ROI to customers, do the customers have any choice but to choose them? They have a responsibility to their stakeholders. Can they really say no to an offer that is clearly a better, more certain investment? Once this shift happens, do Level 2 suppliers still have a choice about crossing over to Level 3 or 4 operating models? Sure, there is risk to both sides by crossing over this line too soon by agreeing to an operating model that neither side can really deliver. But a Level 2 supplier that waits too long takes the risk of getting left behind by a market that has switched how they think about buying technology.

Business Model Implications

Another big thing Level 2 suppliers must do is prepare their cost structure for Levels 3 and 4. If we are right and Level 2 is no longer a permanent state but a transitory one as tech markets mature (see Figure 10.5), then suppliers are going to have some very hard decisions to make. That's because how they make money changes at Levels 3 and 4.

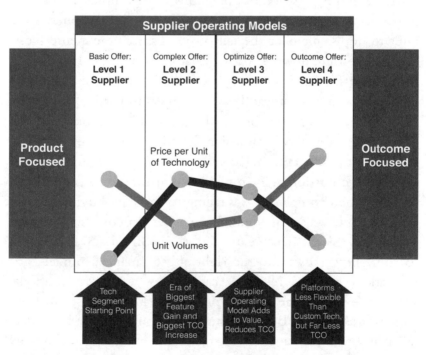

FIGURE 10.5 The Supplier Transformation Challenge of B4B

We just used the CRM market to exemplify how tech offers move from Level 1 to Level 2 to Level 3. It is a fact that the price per unit also changed at each level. Act! cost several hundred bucks. Siebel was a couple million bucks. Level 3 suppliers such as salesforce.com already represent a lower cost-per-license alternative to today's Level 2 offers from SAP and Oracle. If Microsoft had its way, it would probably love to become the first true, fully automated Level 4 CRM supplier. You can bet that would bring everyone's prices down. You can also bet that the unit volumes would go up. Salesforce.com is proving that it can steal market share each and every quarter just by offering a Level 3 solution. So are AWS and Rackspace in their markets. If traditional Level 2 computing and storage companies can't match the prices and value of companies such as these, they risk losing their customers. The best they could hope for is to have two very large customers: AWS and Rackspace. But operating at high unit volumes and lower prices is not what most large Level 2 tech suppliers were built to do. Remember the tail of our fish? The expense (cost) line was heading down. It has to. That can only be achieved by a technology-fueled, data-driven operating model—one that drives labor costs down significantly. For suppliers in particular, moving right on the B4B framework has huge implications on how they conduct business. R&D must significantly redirect their focus far beyond just multi-tenancy. How suppliers sell will change. So will their service portfolios. Even which companies they acquire will change. When complexity was racing to the stars, buying an outsourcer made sense. In hindsight, maybe someone should have bought AWS! We have extended the TSIA B4B framework to show how moving to the right affects financial models, go-to-market models, required capabilities, and organizational structures—more than 20 transformations. These transformations are not insignificant. But we believe they can and must be undertaken in order for suppliers to succeed in maturing technology markets where ROI is the key competing factor.

To be perfectly clear, not every supplier needs to move to the right. Maybe a tech component product manufacturer can remain peacefully in its current Level 1 mode. Maybe an enterprise software company that has found an interesting new niche has another decade of feature-led growth. That is absolutely great. Remaining at Level 2 makes sense. In cases such as these, focusing on improving the operational excellence of their existing operating model is exactly the right thing.

But maybe a supplier senses that its product markets are facing deteriorating core-offer profitability. Or that demand for XaaS is increasing. Or maybe a few of its most important customers are quietly asking the supplier to move its operating model to the right. When any of those are the case, we offer one final tale.

Gulliver and the Lilliputians

These are serious challenges requiring increasingly urgent action, especially for Level 2 suppliers. But the fish problem may be causing them to hesitate. They may feel trapped between what shareholders want in the short term and what customers will want in the long term. But they must avoid the Gulliver Scenario (see Figure 10.6).

Giants Who Sleep Too Long

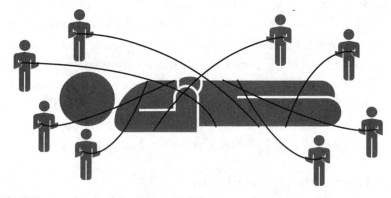

FIGURE 10.6 Giants Who Sleep Too Long

You probably know the story. Gulliver could have easily combated any of the tiny Lilliputians. After all, he was the only giant on the island. But he was asleep. And he slept too long. It was no single Lilliputian who conquered him: It was because one tiny Lilliputian tied down his left foot and another tied down his right one. At the same time, a different group attacked his left arm while yet another was busy on his right. By the time Gulliver finally woke up, it was too late. He had lost his power. And none of it was due to the action of another giant.

Dominant Level 2 suppliers must be vigilant to avoid Gulliver's fate. They can't wait too long to create new operating model capabilities inside their core. They can't dismiss all the little new model companies for too long. They can't pretend that just switching to subscription pricing, and then demanding huge minimum commitments, is their new model. We think shareholders can be made to understand that logic. Successful suppliers must be awake and active about their transformation. They cannot remain still while others take action. Do you agree?

If you do and you are a supplier, you must develop a deadline for adding a new operating model to your repertoire. If you do and you are a business customer, you must develop a deadline for redefining your supplier selection criteria and preparing your internal cost reduction plans. For both sides, the key question is, When? When will the industry's standard operating model in a particular tech sector switch from one level to another? Try this simple exercise: Figure out what supplier level in Figure 10.4 is the standard today for a given tech sector. By what year will the standard be one level further to the right? How many years will it be before you are ready to play at that different level? If your answer to what year the market will move one level right is sooner than the year you will be ready, you may have a problem.

The Next Generation of B2B

In 1884, John H. Patterson sat down with a clean sheet of paper and devised the modern B2B operating model. The complexity of his products necessitated a new approach. It was a triumph of ingenuity and practicality that lasted for 125 years.

Today, we are staring at the hard line that separates his legacy from two new partnership models for suppliers and their customers. Never before was it possible to cross, to conquer complexity in new ways. But today, thanks to the way that software and the Internet have eaten the world, we have the technology and the data and the analytics to double our options for bridging the great divide. New thinking is arriving. New models are developing. New leaders are emerging. They believe that the ROI of technology can be even better than it is today. And customers are responding.

That one line? It could trigger the reinvention of many B2B high-tech and near-tech markets. But it only matters if you agree. Is it time for your company to get ready for B4B?

Epilogue

IF WE WERE A LEVEL 2 CEO WHO WANTED TO EXPLAIN TO EMPLOYEES OR investors the changes facing the company in the era of B4B, here is what we would say:

> *We have built a spectacularly successful company by focusing on great products supported by great services. In some of our product markets, customers are now asking us to do more—to develop an operating model in which we become actively involved in the business outcomes they get from our technology. They also want us to better align our financial results with theirs. For the first time, connected products and data analytics make it possible for us to do that profitably and at scale. Although this model may have some impact on the short-term financial performance of the company, we know it's what our customers want of us, and therefore, it is in the best long-term interest of shareholders.*
>
> *This transformation will require many of you to venture out of your comfort zone. There will be some changes to organizations and job descriptions as we add new offers to our portfolio. However, it does not mean that we are transforming the company in one dramatic shift. Rather, we will begin updating and adding to our corporate capabilities. We will learn new skills and play new roles that help customers realize the full potential of our technology. Soon we will be able to operate profitably in different product markets using different operating models.*
>
> *I would like to turn the meeting over to our COO to explain how we will accomplish this . . .*

We hope this book helps structure a productive, meaningful conversation among all your stakeholders.

Endnotes

Chapter 1

1. J.B. Wood, Todd Hewlin, and Thomas Lah, *Consumption Economics: The New Rules of Tech* (San Diego, CA: Point B, Inc., 2011).

2. "John Henry Patterson 1844-1922: The Biography of the Founder of NCR, Part 1. 1844-1884," NCR, http://www.ncr.org.uk/page107.html.

3. Gerhard Gschwandtner, "John Henry Patterson: The Father of Professional Selling Part I," *Selling Power Blog*, July 13, 2010, http://blog.sellingpower.com/gg/2010/07/john-henry-patterson-the-father-of-professional-selling-part-i.html.

4. Walter A. Friedman, "John H. Patterson and the Sales Strategy of the National Cash Register Company, 1884 to 1922," *Business History Review* 74, no. 4 (Winter 1998): 552–84.

5. Gschwandtner, "John Henry Patterson: Part I."

6. Friedman, "John H. Patterson."

7. Ibid.

8. "John H. Patterson (NCR Owner)," *Wikipedia*, http://en.wikipedia.org/wiki/John_Henry_Patterson_(NCR_owner).

9. Gschwandtner, "John H. Patterson, Part I."

10. "John H. Patterson (NCR Owner)," *Wikipedia*, http://en.wikipedia.org/wiki/John_Henry_Patterson_(NCR_owner).

11. J.B. Wood, *Complexity Avalanche: Overcoming the Threat to Technology Adoption* (San Diego, CA: Point B, Inc., 2009).

12. CFO Research and AlixPartners, *Maximizing the Value of Information Technology: CFOs Dissect their Companies' Spending and Return on IT* (Boston: CFO Publishing, 2013).

13. Ibid.

Chapter 2

1. Sucharita Mulpuru with Carrie Johnson and Douglas Roberge, *U.S. Online Retail Forecast, 2012 to 2017* (Cambridge, MA: Forrester Research, 2013).

2. Ray Wang, "How Intuit Uses Cloud Computing," *Forbes.com*, February 9, 2012, http://www.forbes.com/sites/raywang/2012/02/09/how-intuit-uses-cloud-computing/.

3. John J. Sviokla and Adam J. Gutstein, PwC, "Designing your fiercest competitor: Mastering change by making it real," http://www.pwc.com/us/en/view/issue-15/business-strategy-competitor.jhtml.

Chapter 3

1. TSIA Service 50 Dataview, Q1 2013.

2. The Conference Board Global Economic Outlook 2013, May 2013 update.

3. J.B. Wood, Todd Hewlin, and Thomas Lah, *Consumption Economics: The New Rules of Tech* (San Diego, CA: Point B, Inc., 2011).

4. Ibid.

5. PwC and TSIA, 2012.

Chapter 5

1. Marc Andreessen, "Why Software Is Eating the World," *Wall Street Journal*, August 11, 2011.

2. Emi Doi, "High-Tech Tea Kettle Gives Some Seniors a Sense of Security," *Knight Ridder*, April 8, 2005, http://bullnotbull.com/special/special-5.html.

3. Peter C. Evans and Marco Annunziata, *Industrial Internet: Pushing the Boundaries of Minds and Machines* (white paper, GE, November 26, 2012), http://www.ge.com/docs/chapters/Industrial_Internet.pdf.

4. David Whelan, "What Business Can Learn from Cleveland Clinic: How to Report Quality to the Public," *Forbes.com*, September 2, 2012, http://www.forbes.com/sites/davidwhelan/2012/09/02/what-business-can-learn-from-cleveland-clinic-how-to-report-quality-to-the-public/.

Chapter 6

1. "HP to Acquire EDS for $13.9 Billion" (press release), *hp.com*, May 13, 2008, http://www8.hp.com/us/en/hp-news/press-release.html?id=169924#.Ue4FFY1vMa4.

2. "Xerox to Acquire Affiliated Computer Services" (press release), *Xerox.com*, September 28, 2009, http://news.xerox.com/news/NR_2009Sept28_Xerox_to_Acquire_ACS.

3. J.B. Wood, *Complexity Avalanche* (San Diego, CA: Point B, Inc., 2009).

Chapter 7

1. "Solution selling," http://wikipedia.org/wiki/Solution_selling.

2. For more on provocation-based selling, check out the article coauthored by Philip Lay, Todd Hewlin, and Geoffrey Moore, "In a Downturn, Provoke Your Customers," *Harvard Business Review*, March 2009, http://hbr.org/2009/03/in-a-downturn-provoke-your-customers/ar/1.

3. J.B. Wood, Todd Hewlin, and Thomas Lah, *Consumption Economics: The New Rules of Tech* (San Diego, CA: Point B, Inc., 2011).

4. Ibid.

Chapter 8

1. J.B. Wood, Todd Hewlin, and Thomas Lah, *Consumption Economics: The New Rules of Tech* (San Diego, CA: Point B, Inc., 2011).

Index